A
Christmas
Reader

A
Christmas
Reader

COMPILED BY
Gail Harvey

GRAMERCY BOOKS

NEW YORK · AVENEL, NEW JERSEY

Introduction
Copyright © 1993 by Outlet Book Company, Inc.
All rights reserved

This 1993 edition is published by Gramercy Books,
distributed by Outlet Book Company, Inc.
a Random House Company,
40 Engelhard Avenue
Avenel, New Jersey 07001

Random House
New York • Toronto • London • Sydney • Auckland

Designed by Liz Trovato

Printed and bound in the United States of America

Library of Congress Cataloging-in-Publication Data
A Christmas reader.
p.   cm.
ISBN 0-517-09338-3
1. Christmas—Literary collections.   I. Gramercy Books (Firm)
PN6071.C6C558   1993
808.8'033—dc20   93-15526
CIP

8 7 6 5 4 3 2 1

Contents

Introduction

CHRISTMAS is a magical season and many writers have described the delights of its cherished traditions and recalled warm memories of holidays past. This is a new collection of time-honored stories and recollections to enhance your celebrations today and in the years ahead.

The Burglar's Christmas by Willa Cather is a touching story that reflects her own deep spiritual values. *The Gift of Love* is Georgene Faulkner's charming re-creation of the wonder of the shepherds on the night "the promised King" was born. Included, too, is her charming retelling of the legend of St. Nicholas and Clement C. Moore's perennial favorite *A Visit from St. Nicholas*.

The beginning of *Little Women* by Louisa May Alcott stands alone as a story of a loving and generous Christmas, despite the hardships imposed by a war—the Civil War. Most of Sarah Orne Jewett's stories are set in her beloved Maine, as is the Christmas tale included here—*Mrs. Parkin's Christmas Eve*—which tells of the transformation of a parsimonious old lady. Charles Dickens' description of a Victorian Christmas day reminds us that the family spirit has changed little through the years.

And, of course, no holiday anthology would be complete without O. Henry's moving story *Gifts of the Magi*, Hans Christian Andersen's thought-provoking tale *The Little Fir Tree*, Washington Irving's *Christmas Thoughts*, or the editorial which originally appeared in *The New York Sun—Is There a Santa Claus?*

It is hoped that this *Christmas Reader* will enrich the holiday season for you, your family, and friends and will, in the words of Robert Louis Stevenson, help you "share in the song of the angels, the gladness of the shepherds, and the worship of the wise men."

GAIL HARVEY

The Gift of Love

GEORGENE FAULKNER

I T WAS A COLD NIGHT for that part of the world, and the shepherds who were out watching their flocks upon the hillside drew their heavy cloaks about them. They had built a campfire to give them warmth and as they sat in a group about the bright blaze they told stories to each other.

"You speak of the coming of the King, Grandsire," said a young shepherd boy eagerly as he leaned toward an old man who was talking. "Tell us more about the King."

"Yes, boy," answered the old man, "I will tell you the tale as my mother told it to me.

"Long, long ago, there was a shepherd boy named David who wandered on these very hills near Bethlehem, keeping watch over his father's sheep. David heard the story of the promised King who was to be sent from God to rule over all his people. David was so happy that he played upon his harp, and as he led the sheep through the green pastures and beside the still waters he sang of God as the Heavenly Shepherd.

"When David grew up to be a man he became a king and wore royal robes and a golden crown upon his head and he ruled over all the people. After David came King Solomon, and no king could rival the grandeur of his palace and court. Since then many kings have ruled over us, but the promised King has not come upon the earth, and the songs of David have not yet been fulfilled."

"Oh, how I wish that I might see the King!" said the boy earnestly.

"You are young, boy, and—who knows? Maybe you will live to see the time when these prophecies come true. But I am old and weary with waiting and working and I may never live to see the promised King. Yet I know that the word of God will come true and that He will send His only beloved son to rule the earth."

As the wind whistled over the hillside the sheep huddled more closely together.

"Our little lambs will suffer with the cold," said the shepherd boy.

"No," answered his father, "look at the way the mother sheep lie closely about them, protecting the lambs with their warm bodies. No, the old sheep may feel the chill wind but they will not let their babies suffer."

"Just look at my little baby lamb," said the boy. "See, it is curled up snugly by its mother. Oh! I do hope that no harm will come to it, for it is the tiniest lamb of the flock and I love it. Do you know, Father, I call it Snow-White, for it is like the white snow which we sometimes see on the far distant mountain peaks."

"Come, boy," said the father, "you have rested all day, so you watch the flock and the fire for a time and I will lie down here by Grandsire and take a nap."

The boy lay upon the ground looking at the campfire smoke curling up toward the sky. Then he looked at the sleeping shepherds stretched out upon the ground, and as his eyes rested upon the old man he remembered the story and said softly, "How I should like to see that King!"

The cold wind seemed to die down and the clouds went across the sky like a flock of scurrying sheep, leaving the stars twinkling brightly in the dark-blue vault of the heavens.

"How beautiful it is, and how still!" he said.

He looked again at the group of sleeping shepherds, and then he looked at the sleeping sheep. As he watched, he saw his little lamb stir uneasily.

"Poor little baby, poor little Snow White, I believe that it is lonely. I will hold it under my warm coat and protect it while the mother sheep sleeps." And so the boy lifted the baby lamb in his strong arms and, opening his coat, he held it closely to him, while the mother sheep slept peacefully by his side. The boy forgot to watch the fire and it soon flickered and went out.

He felt a strange chill over all the land, and it was so still—so very still that he wished the men would awaken, or that one of the sheep would bleat, for he felt lonely and afraid and he knew not why.

Suddenly he saw a bright light flashing through the heavens. Was he asleep or dreaming? He sat up and rubbed his eyes. No, the

light was coming nearer and nearer, down, down toward the earth. Then he saw that the sheep were stirring uneasily and he heard them bleating, for they were frightened from their sleep. The shepherds, too, were awakening.

"What is the meaning of this strange light?" said one.

"Has a star fallen from the sky?" asked another.

"See this golden cloud of glory resting over us. It is so dazzling bright that I dare not look upon it."

The shepherds seized their staffs and some of them covered their faces with their cloaks, for they were very frightened. The old man went down upon his knees and looked up reverently while the boy stood motionless gazing spellbound at the radiant vision, for, as they watched, they saw in this cloud of golden glory a beautiful angel who came down, down to the earth and stood upon the hillside among them. When they saw this messenger from God the shepherds trembled with fear, and the angel said:

"Fear not, for behold, I bring you good tidings which shall be of great joy to all people. For unto you is born this day, in the city of David, a Savior which is Christ the Lord. And this shall be a sign unto you, ye shall find the Babe wrapped in swaddling clothes lying in a manger."

And, as the angel ceased speaking, suddenly the heavens opened and there was with the angel a multitude of the heavenly host who were singing and praising God, saying: "Glory to God in the highest, and on earth peace, good will toward men."

Then the bright light was gone and the startled shepherds looked up long and earnestly toward the sky.

"Truly, it was a message from God," said the old shepherd, as he bowed his white head. "God has sent us this angel to tell us that the promised King has come."

"But the angel said that the Babe was wrapped in swaddling clothes and lying in a manger," said the boy. "Is it not strange for a prince to come to such a lowly place?"

"Yes," said the old man, "it seems strange, but we know that He is truly the gift of love from God—His only Son who has been promised to us for, lo, these many years. I thank God that my old eyes have been permitted to see this heavenly vision. Come, we must go in haste to find Him."

"What gift of love shall we carry to the King, Grandsire?" whispered the boy.

"The most precious thing we own," answered the old man, "that which we love the best."

"But we shepherds have no gold nor silver, nor sparkling gems fit for a king," said one of the shepherds. "What, then, can we carry to this child?"

"I know," said the boy, as he looked lovingly down upon the little lamb which he was still holding in his strong young arms, "we can give this lamb—Snow White. It is the purest and whitest little lamb from our flock. I love it and it is the best that we have to offer, and surely the good Father in Heaven knows that we are bringing our gift of love to the King."

"The boy is right," said the old man. "This baby lamb—the purest of the flock—is truly our gift of love."

And so the shepherds went in haste down the hillside, the boy holding in his arms the baby lamb. Once it bleated softly, "Ma-Ma-a-a," as though it called its mother, and the boy seemed to hear the mother sheep on the hillside calling out, "Ba-ba-a-a," as though she were calling her baby.

"Poor mother sheep, she will be grieving for her little one," said the boy to himself. "But if she could only understand she would be glad to give her lamb to the King."

At last they reached the little town of Bethlehem, and they came to a low stable built upon the hillside, and there they found their King—a tiny babe wrapped in swaddling clothes, as the angel had said, and lying in a manger.

They saw the cattle standing near and Joseph watching over the Holy Mother Mary and the Heavenly Child.

This was no palace home, these were no royal robes of state. But the shepherds knew that the words of the angel were true and that this Babe was their promised King. The heavenly light was streaming from the face of the Holy Child and the shepherds covered their faces, for they could not look upon its radiance. Then they fell upon their knees and worshipped the Child, and thanked God that the gift of love had been given to all the waiting world.

The boy looked on with wondering eyes, and then he held out the little lamb, and the Babe smiled into the eyes of the boy and stretched out His tiny hands as though He would take the lamb. Then the boy sank slowly down upon his knees by the Babe and placed at His feet the tiniest lamb from the flock—a gift of love for the Christ Child.

Gifts of the Magi

O. HENRY

O NE DOLLAR AND EIGHTY-SEVEN CENTS. That was all. And sixty cents of it was in pennies. Pennies saved one and two at a time by bulldozing the grocer and the vegetable man and the butcher until one's cheeks burned with the silent imputation of parsimony that such close dealing implied. Three times Della counted it. One dollar and eighty-seven cents. And the next day would be Christmas.

There was clearly nothing to do but flop down on the shabby little couch and howl. So Della did it. Which instigates the moral reflection that life is made up of sobs, sniffles, and smiles, with sniffles predominating.

While the mistress of the home is gradually subsiding from the first stage to the second, take a look at the home. A furnished flat at eight dollars per week. It did not exactly beggar description, but it certainly had that word on the lookout for the mendicancy squad.

In the vestibule below was a letter box into which no letter would go, and an electric button from which no mortal finger could coax a ring. Also appertaining thereunto was a card bearing the name "Mr. James Dillingham Young."

The "Dillingham" had been flung to the breeze during a former period of prosperity when its possessor was being paid thirty dollars per week. Now, when the income was shrunk to twenty dollars, the letters of "Dillingham" looked blurred, as though they were thinking seriously of contracting to a modest and unassuming D. But whenever Mr. James Dillingham Young came home and reached his flat above he was called "Jim" and greatly hugged by Mrs. James Dillingham Young, already introduced to you as Della. Which is all very good.

Della finished her cry and attended to her cheeks with the powder rag. She stood by the window and looked out dully at a gray cat walking a gray fence in a gray backyard. Tomorrow would be

Christmas Day, and she had only one dollar and eighty-seven cents with which to buy Jim a present. She had been saving every penny she could for months, with this result. Twenty dollars a week doesn't go far. Expenses had been greater than she had calculated. They always are. Only one dollar and eighty-seven cents to buy a present for Jim. Her Jim. Many a happy hour she had spent planning for something nice for him. Something fine and rare and sterling—something just a little bit near to being worthy of the honor of being owned by Jim.

There was a pier glass between the windows of the room. Perhaps you have seen a pier glass in an eight-dollar flat. A very thin and very agile person may, by observing his reflection in a rapid sequence of longitudinal strips, obtain a fairly accurate conception of his looks. Della, being slender, had mastered the art.

Suddenly she whirled from the window and stood before the glass. Her eyes were shining brilliantly, but her face had lost its color within twenty seconds. Rapidly she pulled down her hair and let it fall to its full length.

Now, there were two possessions of the James Dillingham Youngs in which they both took a mighty pride. One was Jim's gold watch that had been his father's and grandfather's. The other was Della's hair. Had the Queen of Sheba lived in the flat across the air shaft, Della would have let her hair hang out the window some day to dry just to depreciate her majesty's jewels and gifts. Had King Solomon been the janitor, with all his treasures piled up in the basement, Jim would have pulled out his watch every time he passed, just to see him pluck at his beard from envy.

So now Della's beautiful hair fell about her, rippling and shining like a cascade of brown waters. It reached below her knee and made itself almost a garment for her. And then she did it up again nervously and quickly. Once she faltered for a minute and stood still while a tear or two splashed on the worn red carpet.

On went her old brown jacket; on went her old brown hat. With a whirl of skirts and with the brilliant sparkle still in her eyes, she fluttered out the door and down the stairs to the street.

Where she stopped the sign read: "Mme. Sofronie. Hair Goods of

All Kinds." One flight up Della ran, and collected herself, panting. Madame, large, too white, chilly, hardly looked the "Sofronie."

"Will you buy my hair?" asked Della.

"I buy hair," said Madame. "Take yer hat off and let's have a sight at the looks of it."

Down rippled the brown cascade.

"Twenty dollars," said Madame, lifting the mass with a practiced hand.

"Give it to me quick," said Della.

Oh, and the next two hours tripped by on rosy wings. Forget the hashed metaphor. She was ransacking the stores for Jim's present.

She found it at last. It surely had been made for Jim and no one else. There was no other like it in any of the stores, and she had turned all of them inside out. It was a platinum fob chain simple and chaste in design, properly proclaiming its value by substance alone and not by meretricious ornamentation—as all good things should do. It was even worthy of The Watch. As soon as she saw it she knew that it must be Jim's. It was like him. Quietness and value—the description applied to both. Twenty-one dollars they took from her for it, and she hurried home with the eighty-seven cents. With that chain on his watch Jim might be properly anxious about the time in any company. Grand as the watch was, he sometimes looked at it on the sly on account of the old leather strap that he used in place of a chain.

When Della reached home her intoxication gave way a little to prudence and reason. She got out her curling irons and lighted the gas and went to work repairing the ravages made by generosity added to love. Which is always a tremendous task, dear friends—a mammoth task.

Within forty minutes her head was covered with tiny, close-lying curls that made her look wonderfully like a truant schoolboy. She looked at her reflection in the mirror long, carefully, and critically.

"If Jim doesn't kill me," she said to herself, "before he takes a second look at me, he'll say I look like a Coney Island chorus girl. But what could I do—oh! what could I do with a dollar and eighty-seven cents?"

At seven o'clock the coffee was made and the frying pan was on the back of the stove and ready to cook the chops.

Jim was never late. Della doubled the fob chain in her hand and sat on the corner of the table near the door that he always entered. Then she heard his step on the stair away down on the first flight, and she turned white for just a moment. She had a habit of saying little silent prayers about the simplest everyday things, and now she whispered: "Please God, make him think I am still pretty."

The door opened and Jim stepped in and closed it. He looked thin and very serious. Poor fellow, he was only twenty-two—and to be burdened with a family! He needed a new overcoat and he was without gloves.

Jim stopped inside the door, as immovable as a setter at the scent of quail. His eyes were fixed upon Della, and there was an expression in them that she could not read, and it terrified her. It was not anger, nor surprise, nor disapproval, nor horror, nor any of the sentiments that she had been prepared for. He simply stared at her fixedly with that peculiar expression on his face.

Della wriggled off the table and went for him.

"Jim, darling," she cried, "don't look at me that way. I had my hair cut off and sold it because I couldn't have lived through Christmas without giving you a present. It'll grow out again—you won't mind, will you? I just had to do it. My hair grows awfully fast. Say 'Merry Christmas!' Jim, and let's be happy. You don't know what a nice— what a beautiful, nice gift I've got for you."

"You've cut off your hair?" asked Jim, laboriously, as if he had not arrived at that patent fact yet even after the hardest mental labor.

"Cut it off and sold it," said Della. "Don't you like me just as well, anyhow? I'm me without my hair, ain't I?"

Jim looked about the room curiously.

"You say your hair is gone?" he said, with an air almost of idiocy.

"You needn't look for it," said Della. "It's sold, I tell you—sold and gone, too. It's Christmas Eve, boy. Be good to me, for it went for you. Maybe the hairs of my head were numbered," she went on with a sudden serious sweetness, "but nobody could ever count my love for you. Shall I put the chops on, Jim?"

Out of his trance Jim seemed quickly to wake. He enfolded his Della. For ten seconds let us regard with discreet scrutiny some inconsequential object in the other direction. Eight dollars a week or a million a year—what is the difference? A mathematician or a wit would give you the wrong answer. The magi brought valuable gifts, but that was not among them. This dark assertion will be illuminated later on.

Jim drew a package from his overcoat pocket and threw it upon the table.

"Don't make any mistake, Dell," he said, "about me. I don't think there's anything in the way of a haircut or a shave or a shampoo that could make me like my girl any less. But if you'll unwrap that package you may see why you had me going a while at first."

White fingers and nimble tore at the string and paper. And then an ecstatic scream of joy; and then, alas! a quick feminine change to hysterical tears and wails, necessitating the immediate employment of all the comforting powers of the lord of the flat.

For there lay The Combs—the set of combs, side and back, that Della had worshiped for long in a Broadway window. Beautiful combs, pure tortoise shell, with jeweled rims—just the shade to wear in the beautiful vanished hair. They were expensive combs, she knew, and her heart had simply craved and yearned over them without the least hope of possession. And now, they were hers, but the tresses that should have adorned the coveted adornments were gone.

But she hugged them to her bosom, and at length she was able to look up with dim eyes and a smile and say: "My hair grows so fast, Jim!"

And then Della leaped up like a little singed cat and cried, "Oh, oh!"

Jim had not yet seen his beautiful present. She held it out to him eagerly upon her open palm. The dull precious metal seemed to flash with a reflection of her bright and ardent spirit.

"Isn't it a dandy, Jim? I hunted all over town to find it. You'll have to look at the time a hundred times a day now. Give me your watch. I want to see how it looks on it."

Instead of obeying, Jim tumbled down on the couch and put his hands under the back of his head and smiled.

"Dell," said he, "let's put our Christmas presents away and keep 'em a while. They're too nice to use just at present. I sold the watch to get the money to buy your combs. And now suppose you put the chops on."

The magi, as you know, were wise men—wonderfully wise men who brought gifts to the Babe in the manger. They invented the art of giving Christmas presents. Being wise, their gifts were no doubt wise ones, possibly bearing the privilege of exchange in case of duplication. And here I have lamely related to you the uneventful chronicle of two foolish children in a flat who most unwisely sacrificed for each other the greatest treasures of their house. But, in a last word to the wise of these days, let it be said that of all who give gifts these two were the wisest. Of all who give and receive gifts, such as they are wisest. Everywhere they are wisest. They are the magi.

The Burglar's Christmas

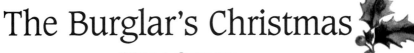

WILLA CATHER

Two very shabby-looking young men stood at the corner of Prairie Avenue and Eightieth Street, looking despondently at the carriages that whirled by. It was Christmas Eve, and the streets were full of vehicles: florists' wagons, grocers' carts, and carriages. The streets were in that half-liquid, half-congealed condition peculiar to the streets of Chicago at that season of the year. The swift wheels that spun by sometimes threw the slush of mud and snow over the two young men who were talking on the corner.

"Well," remarked the elder of the two, "I guess we are at our rope's end, sure enough. How do you feel?"

"Pretty shaky. The wind's sharp tonight. If I had had anything to eat I mightn't mind it so much. There is simply no show. I'm sick of the whole business. Looks like there's nothing for it but the lake."

"Oh, nonsense, I thought you had more grit. Got anything left you can hock?"

"Nothing but my beard, and I am afraid they wouldn't find it worth a pawn ticket," said the younger man ruefully, rubbing the week's growth of stubble on his face.

"Got any folks anywhere? Now's your time to strike 'em if you have."

"Never mind if I have, they're out of the question."

"Well, you'll be out of it before many hours if you don't make a move of some sort. A man's got to eat. See here, I am going down to Longtin's saloon. I used to play the banjo in there and I'll bone him for some of his free-lunch stuff. You'd better come along. Perhaps they'll fill an order for two."

"How far down is it?"

"Well, it's clear downtown, of course, 'way down on Michigan Avenue."

"Thanks, I guess I'll loaf around here. I don't feel equal to the walk, and the cars—well, the cars are crowded." His features drew them-

19

selves into what might have been a smile under happier circumstances.

"No, you never did like streetcars, you're too aristocratic. See here, Crawford, I don't like leaving you here. You ain't good company for yourself tonight."

"Crawford? Oh, yes, that's the last one. There have been so many I forget them."

"Have you got a real name, anyway?"

"Oh, yes, but it's one of the ones I've forgotten. Don't you worry about me. You go along and get your free lunch. I think I had a row in Longtin's place once. I'd better not show myself there again." As he spoke the young man nodded and turned slowly up the avenue.

He was miserable enough to want to be quite alone. Even the crowd that jostled by him annoyed him. He wanted to think about himself. He had avoided this final reckoning with himself for a year now. He had laughed it off and drunk it off. But now, when all those artificial devices which are employed to turn our thoughts into other channels and shield us from ourselves had failed him, it must come. Hunger is a powerful incentive to introspection.

It is a tragic hour, that hour when we are finally driven to reckon with ourselves, when every avenue of mental distraction has been cut off and our own life and all its ineffaceable failures closes about us like the walls of that old torture chamber of the Inquisition. Tonight, as this man stood stranded in the streets of the city, his hour came. It was not the first time he had been hungry and desperate and alone. But always before there had been some outlook, some chance ahead, some pleasure yet untasted that seemed worth the effort, some face that he fancied was, or would be, dear. But it was not so tonight. The unyielding conviction was upon him that he had failed in everything, had outlived everything. It had been near him for a long time, that Pale Specter. He had caught its shadow at the bottom of his glass many a time, at the head of his bed when he was sleepless at night, in the twilight shadows when some great sunset broke upon him. It had made life hateful to him when he awoke in the morning before now. But now it settled slowly over him, like night, the endless Northern nights that bid the sun a long farewell. It rose up before him like granite. From this brilliant city with its glad bustle of Yuletide he was shut off as completely as though he were a creature of another species. His days seemed numbered and done, sealed over like the little coral cells at the bottom of the sea. Involuntarily he drew that cold air through his lungs slowly, as though he were tasting it for the last time.

Yet he was but four and twenty, this man—he looked even younger—and he had a father some place down East who had been very proud of him once. Well, he had taken his life into his own hands, and this was what he had made of it. That was all there was to be said. He could remember the hopeful things they used to say about him at college in the old days, before he had cut away and begun to live by his wits, and he found courage to smile at them now. They had read him wrongly. He knew now that he never had the essentials of success, only the superficial agility that is often mistaken for it. He was tow without the tinder, and he had burnt himself out at other people's fires. He had helped other people to make it win, but he himself—he had never touched an enterprise that had not failed eventually. Or, if it survived his connection with it, it left him behind.

His last venture had been with some ten-cent specialty company, a little lower than all the others, that had gone to pieces in Buffalo, and he had worked his way to Chicago by boat. When the boat made up its crew for the outward voyage, he was dispensed with as usual. He was used to that. The reason for it? Oh, there are so many reasons for failure! His was a very common one.

As he stood there in the wet under the streetlight, he drew up his reckoning with the world and decided that it had treated him as well as he deserved. He had overdrawn his account once too often. There had been a day when he thought otherwise, when he had said he was unjustly handled, that his failure was merely the lack of proper adjustment between himself and other men, that some day he would be recognized and it would all come right. But he knew better than that now, and he was still man enough to bear no grudge against anyone—man or woman.

Tonight was his birthday, too. There seemed something particularly amusing in that. He turned up a limp coat collar to try to keep a little of the wet chill from his throat, and instinctively began to remember all the birthday parties he used to have. He was so cold and empty that his mind seemed unable to grapple with any serious questions. He kept thinking about gingerbread and frosted cakes, like a child. He could remember the splendid birthday parties his mother used to give him, when all the other little boys in the block came in their Sunday clothes and creaking shoes, with their ears still red from their mother's towel, and the pink and white birthday cake, and the stuffed olives and all the dishes of which he had been particularly fond, and how he would eat and eat and then go to bed and dream of Santa Claus. And in the morning he would awaken and eat again, until by night the family doctor arrived with his castor oil, and poor William used to dolefully say that it was altogether too much to have your birthday and Christmas all at once. He could remember, too, the royal birthday suppers he had given at college, and the stag dinners, and the toasts, and the music, and the good fellows who had wished him happiness and really meant what they said.

And since then there were other birthday suppers that he could not remember so clearly; the memory of them was heavy and flat, like cigarette smoke that has been shut in a room all night, like champagne that has been a day opened, a song that has been too often sung, an acute sensation that has been overstrained. They seemed tawdry and garish, discordant to him now. He rather wished he could forget them altogether.

Whichever way his mind now turned, there was one thought that it could not escape, and that was the idea of food. He caught the scent of a cigar suddenly, and felt a sharp pain in the pit of his abdomen and a sudden moisture in his mouth. His cold hands clenched angrily, and for a moment he felt that bitter hatred of wealth, of ease, of everything that is well fed and well housed that is common to starving men. At any rate he had a right to eat! He had demanded great things from the world once: fame and wealth and admiration. Now it was simply bread—and he would have it! He looked about him quickly and felt the blood begin to stir in his veins. In all his straits he had never stolen anything; his tastes were above it. But tonight there would be no tomorrow. He was amused at the way in which the idea excited him. Was it possible there was yet one more experience that would distract him, one thing that had power to excite his jaded interest? Good! He had failed at everything else, now he would see what his chances would be as a common thief. It would be amusing to watch the beautiful consistency of his destiny work itself out even in that role. It would be interesting to add another study to his gallery of futile attempts, and then label them all: "the failure as a journalist," "the failure as a lecturer," "the failure as a businessman," "the failure as a thief," and so on, like the titles under the pictures of the Dance of Death. It was time that Childe Roland came to the dark tower.

A girl hastened by him with her arms full of packages. She walked quickly and nervously, keeping well within the shadow, as if she were not accustomed to carrying bundles and did not care to meet any of her friends. As she crossed the muddy street, she made an effort to lift her skirt a little, and as she did so one of the packages slipped unnoticed from beneath her arm. He caught it up and overtook her. "Excuse me, but I think you dropped something."

She started, "Oh, yes, thank you, I would rather have lost anything than that."

The young man turned angrily upon himself. The package must have contained something of value. Why had he not kept it? Was this the sort of thief he would make? He ground his teeth together. There is nothing more maddening than to have morally consented to crime and than lack the nerve force to carry it out.

A carriage drove up to the house before which he stood. Several richly dressed women alighted and went in. It was a new house, and must have been built since he was in Chicago last. The front door was open and he could see down the hallway and up the staircase. The servant had left the door and gone with the guests. The first floor was brilliantly lighted, but the windows upstairs were dark. It looked very easy, just to slip upstairs to the darkened chambers where the jewels and trinkets of the fashionable occupants were kept.

Still burning with impatience against himself he entered quickly. Instinctively he removed his mud-stained hat as he passed quickly and quietly up the staircase. It struck him as being a rather superfluous courtesy in a burglar, but he had done it before he had thought. His way was clear enough; he met no one on the stairway or in the upper hall. The gas was lit in the upper hall. He passed the first chamber door through sheer cowardice. The second he entered quickly, thinking of something else lest his courage should fail him, and closed the door behind him. The light from the hall shone into the room through the transom. The apartment was furnished richly enough to justify his expectations. He went at once to the dressing case. A number of rings and small trinkets lay in a silver tray. These he put hastily in his pocket. He opened the upper drawer and found, as he expected, several leather cases. In the first he opened was a lady's watch, in the second a pair of old-fashioned bracelets; he seemed to dimly remember having seen bracelets like them before, somewhere. The third case was heavier, the spring was much worn, and it opened easily. It held a cup of some kind. He held it up to the light and then his strained nerves gave way and he uttered a sharp exclamation. It was the silver mug he used to drink from when he was a little boy.

The door opened, and a woman stood in the doorway facing him. She was a tall woman, with white hair, in evening dress. The light from the hall streamed in upon him, but she was not afraid. She stood looking at him a moment, then she threw out her hand and went quickly toward him.

"Willie, Willie ! Is it you?"

He struggled to loose her arms from him, to keep her lips from his cheek. "Mother—you must not! You do not understand! Oh, my God, this is worst of all!" Hunger, weakness, cold, shame, all came back to him, and shook his self-control completely. Physically he was too weak to stand a shock like this. Why could it not have been an ordinary discovery, arrest, the station house and all the rest of it. Anything but this! A hard dry sob broke from him. Again he strove to disengage himself.

"Who is it says I shall not kiss my son? Oh, my boy, we have waited so long for this! You have been so long in coming, even I almost gave you up."

Her lips upon his cheek burned him like fire. He put his hand to his throat, and spoke thickly and incoherently: "You do not understand. I did not know you were here. I came here to rob—it is the first time—I swear it—but I am a common thief. My pockets are full of your jewels now. Can't you hear me? I am a common thief!"

"Hush, my boy, those are ugly words. How could you rob your own house? How could you take what is your own? They are all yours, my son, as wholly yours as my great love—and you can't doubt that, Will, do you?"

That soft voice, the warmth and fragrance of her person stole through his chill, empty veins like a gentle stimulant. He felt as though all his strength were leaving him and even consciousness. He held fast to her and bowed his head on her strong shoulder, and groaned aloud.

"Oh, Mother, life is hard, hard!"

She said nothing, but held him closer. And Oh, the strength of those white arms that held him! Oh, the assurance of safety in that warm bosom that rose and fell under his cheek! For a moment they stood so, silently. Then they heard a heavy step upon the stair. She led him to a chair and went out and closed the door. At the top of the staircase she met a tall, broad-shouldered man, with iron-gray hair, and a face alert and stern. Her eyes were shining and her cheeks on fire, her whole face was one expression of intense determination.

"James, it is William in there, come home. You must keep him at any cost. If he goes this time, I go with him. Oh, James, be easy with him, he has suffered so." She broke from a command to an entreaty, and laid her hand on his shoulder. He looked questioningly at her a moment, then went in the room and quietly shut the door.

She stood leaning against the wall, clasping her temples with her hands and listening to the low indistinct sound of the voices within. Her own lips moved silently. She waited a long time, scarcely breathing. At last the door opened, and her husband came out. He stopped to say in a shaken voice, "You go to him now, he will stay. I will go to my room. I will see him again in the morning."

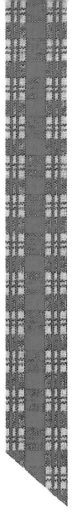

She put her arm about his neck, "Oh, James, I thank you, I thank you! This is the night he came so long ago, you remember? I gave him to you then, and now you give him back to me!"

"Don't, Helen," he muttered. "He is my son, I have never forgotten that. I failed with him. I don't like to fail, it cuts my pride. Take him and make a man of him." He passed on down the hall.

She flew into the room where the young man sat with his head bowed upon his knee. She dropped upon her knees beside him. Ah, it was so good to him to feel those arms again!

"He is so glad, Willie, so glad! He may not show it, but he is as happy as I. He never was demonstrative with either of us, you know."

"Oh, my God, he was good enough," groaned the man. "I told him everything, and he was good enough. I don't see how either of you can look at me, speak to me, touch me." He shivered under her clasp again as when she had first touched him, and tried weakly to throw her off.

But she whispered softly, "This is my right, my son."

Presently, when he was calmer, she rose. "Now, come with me into the library, and I will have your dinner brought there."

As they went downstairs she remarked apologetically, "I will not call Ellen tonight; she has a number of guests to attend to. She is a big girl now, you know, and came out last winter. Besides, I want you all to myself tonight."

When the dinner came, and it came very soon, he fell upon it savagely. As he ate she told him all that had transpired during the years of his absence, and how his father's business had brought them there. "I was glad when we came. I thought you would drift West. I seemed a good deal nearer to you here."

There was a gentle unobtrusive sadness in her tone that was too soft for a reproach.

"Have you everything you want? It is a comfort to see you eat."

He smiled grimly, "It is certainly a comfort to me. I have not indulged in this frivolous habit for some thirty-five hours."

She caught his hand and pressed it sharply, uttering a quick remonstrance.

"Don't say that! I know, but I can't hear you say it—it's too terrible! My boy, food has choked me many a time when I have thought of the possibility of that. Now take the old lounging chair by the fire, and if you are too tired to talk, we will just sit and rest together."

He sank into the depths of the big leather chair with the lions' heads on the arms, where he had sat so often in the days when his feet did not touch the floor and he was half afraid of the grim monsters cut in the polished wood. That chair seemed to speak to him of things long forgotten. It was like the touch of an old familiar friend. He felt a sudden yearning tenderness for the happy little boy who had sat there and dreamed of the big world so long ago. Alas, he had been dead many a summer, that little boy!

He sat looking up at the magnificent woman beside him. He had almost forgotten how handsome she was; how lustrous and sad were the eyes that were set under the serene brow, how impetuous and wayward the mouth even now, how superb the white throat and shoulders! Ah, the wit and grace and fineness of this woman! He remembered how proud he had been of her as a boy when she came to see him at school. Then in the deep red coals of the grate he saw the faces of other women who had come since then into his vexed, disordered life. Laughing faces, with eyes artificially bright, eyes without depth or meaning, features without the stamp of high sensibilities. And he had left this face for such as those!

He sighed restlessly and laid his hand on hers. There seemed refuge and protection in the touch of her, as in the old days when he was afraid of the dark. He had been in the dark so long now, his confidence was so thoroughly shaken, and he was bitterly afraid of the night and of himself.

"Ah, Mother, you make other things seem so false. You must feel that I owe you an explanation, but I can't make any, even to myself. Ah, but we make poor exchanges in life. I can't make out the riddle of it all. Yet, there are things I ought to tell you before I accept your confidence like this."

"I'd rather you wouldn't, Will. Listen: between you and me there can be no secrets. We are more alike than other people. Dear boy, I know all about it. I am a woman, and circumstances were different with me, but we are of one blood. I have lived all your life before you. You have never had an impulse that I have not known, you have never touched a brink that my feet have not trod. This is your birthday night. Twenty-four years ago I foresaw all this. I was a young woman then and I had hot battles of my own, and I felt your likeness to me. You were not like other babies. From the hour you were born you were restless and discontented, as I had been before you. You used to brace your strong little limbs against mine and try to throw me off as you did tonight. Tonight you have come back to me, just as you always did after you ran away to swim in the river that was forbidden you, the river you loved because it was forbidden. You are tired and sleepy, just as you used to be then, only a little older and a little paler and a little more foolish. I never asked you where you had been then, nor will I now. You have come back to me, that's all in all to me. I know your every possibility and limitation, as a composer knows his instrument."

He found no answer that was worthy to give to talk like this. He had not found life easy since he had lived by his wits. He had come to know poverty at close quarters. He had known what it was to be gay with an empty pocket, to wear violets in his buttonhole when he had not breakfasted, and all the hateful shams of the poverty of idleness. He had been a reporter on a big metropolitan daily, where men grind out their brains on paper until they have not one idea left—and still grind on. He had worked in a real estate office, where ignorant men were swindled. He had sung in a comic opera chorus and played Harris in an *Uncle Tom's Cabin* company, and edited a socialist weekly. He had been dogged by debt and hunger and grinding poverty, until to sit here by a warm fire without concern as to how it would be paid for seemed unnatural.

He looked up at her questioningly. "I wonder if you know how much you pardon?"

"Oh, my poor boy, much or little, what does it matter? Have you wandered so far and paid such a bitter price for knowledge and not yet learned that love has nothing to do with pardon or forgiveness, that it only loves, and loves—and loves? They have not taught you

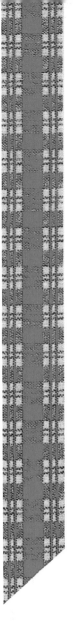

well, the women of your world." She leaned over and kissed him, as no woman had kissed him since he left her.

He drew a long sigh of rich content. The old life, with all its bitterness and useless antagonism and flimsy sophistries, its brief delights that were always tinged with fear and distrust and unfaith, that whole miserable, futile, swindled world of Bohemia seemed immeasurably distant and far away, like a dream that is over and done. And as the chimes rang joyfully outside and sleep pressed heavily upon his eyelids, he wondered dimly if the Author of this sad little riddle of ours were not able to solve it after all, and if the Potter would not finally mete out his all-comprehensive justice, such as none but he could have, to his Things of Clay, which are made in his own patterns, weak or strong, for his own ends; and if some day we will not awaken and find that all evil is a dream, a mental distortion that will pass when the dawn shall break.

A Visit from St. Nicholas

CLEMENT C. MOORE

'T<small>WAS</small> the night before Christmas, when all through the house
Not a creature was stirring, not even a mouse;
The stockings were hung by the chimney with care,
In hopes that St. Nicholas soon would be there.
The children were nestled all snug in their beds,
While visions of sugarplums danced through their heads;

And mamma in her kerchief, and I in my cap,
Had just settled our brains for a long winter's nap—
When out on the lawn there arose such a clatter,
I sprang from my bed to see what was the matter.
Away to the window I flew like a flash,
Tore open the shutters and threw up the sash.
The moon on the breast of the new-fallen snow
Gave the luster of midday to objects below;
When, what to my wondering eyes should appear,
But a miniature sleigh and eight tiny reindeer,
With a little old driver, so lively and quick,
I knew in a moment it must be St. Nick.
More rapid than eagles his coursers they came,
And he whistled, and shouted, and called them by name:

"Now, Dasher! now, Dancer! now, Prancer! and Vixen!
On, Comet! on, Cupid! on, Donder and Blitzen!
To the top of the porch! to the top of the wall!
Now dash away! dash away! dash away all!"
As dry leaves that before the wild hurricane fly,
When they meet with an obstacle, mount to the sky,
So up to the house-top the coursers they flew,
With the sleighful of toys, and St. Nicholas too.
And then in a twinkling I heard on the roof
The prancing and pawing of each little hoof.
As I drew in my head, and was turning around,
Down the chimney St. Nicholas came with a bound.
He was dressed all in fur from his head to his foot,
And his clothes were all tarnished with ashes and soot;
A bundle of toys he had flung on his back,
And he looked like a peddler just opening his pack.
His eyes, how they twinkled! his dimples, how merry!
His cheeks were like roses, his nose like a cherry!
His droll little mouth was drawn up like a bow,
And the beard on his chin was as white as the snow.
The stump of a pipe he held tight in his teeth,
And the smoke, it encircled his head like a wreath.
He had a broad face, and a little round belly
That shook when he laughed, like a bowl full of jelly.
He was chubby and plump—a right jolly old elf;
And I laughed when I saw him, in spite of myself.
A wink of his eye, and a twist of his head
Soon gave me to know I had nothing to dread.
He spoke not a word, but went straight to his work,
And filled all the stockings; then turned with a jerk,
And laying his finger aside of his nose,
And giving a nod, up the chimney he rose.
He sprang to his sleigh, to the team gave a whistle,
And away they all flew, like the down of a thistle,
But I heard him exclaim, ere he drove out of sight,
"Happy Christmas to all, and to all a good night!"

Mrs. Parkins' Christmas Eve

SARAH ORNE JEWETT

I

ONE WINTRY-LOOKING AFTERNOON the sun was getting low, but still shone with cheerful radiance into Mrs. Lydia Parkins' sitting room. To point out a likeness between the bareness of the room and the appearance of the outside world on that twenty-first of December might seem ungracious; but there was a certain leaflessness and inhospitality common to both.

The cold, gray wallpaper, and dull, thin furniture; the indescribable poverty and lack of comfort of the room were exactly like the leaflessness and sharpness and coldness of that early winter day—unless the sun shone out with a golden glow as it had done in the latter part of the afternoon; then both the room and the long hillside and frozen road and distant western hills were quite transfigured.

Mrs. Parkins sat upright in one of the six decorous wooden chairs with cane seats; she was trimming a dismal gray-and-black winter bonnet and her workbasket was on the end of the table in front of her, between the windows, with à row of spools on the windowsill at her left. The only luxury she permitted herself was a cricket, a little bench such as one sees in a church pew, with a bit of carpet to cover its top. Mrs. Parkins was so short that she would have been quite off-roundings otherwise in her cane-seated chair; but she had a great horror of persons who put their feet on chair rungs and wore the paint off. She was always on the watch to break the young of this bad habit. She cast a suspicious glance now and then at little Lucy Deems, who sat in another cane-seated chair opposite. The child had called upon Mrs. Parkins before, and was now trying so hard to be good that both her feet had gone to sleep and had come to the prickling stage of that misery. She wondered if her mother were not almost ready to go home.

Mrs. Deems sat in the rocking chair, full in the sunlight and faced the sun itself, unflinchingly. She was a broad-faced gay-hearted, little woman, and her face was almost as bright as the winter sun itself. One might fancy that they were having a match at trying to outshine one another, but so far it was not Mrs. Deems who blinked and withdrew from the contest. She was just now conscious of little Lucy's depression and anxious looks, and bade her go out to run about a little while and see if there were some of Mrs. Parkins' butternuts left under the big tree.

The door closed, and Mrs. Parkins snapped her thread and said that there was no butternuts out there; perhaps Lucy should have a few in a basket when she was going home.

"Oh, 'taint no matter," said Mrs. Deems, easily. "She was kind of distressed sittin' so quiet; they like to rove about, children does."

"She won't do no mischief?" asked the hostess, timidly.

"Lucy?" laughed the mother. "Why you ought to be better acquainted with Lucy than that, I'm sure. I catch myself wishing she wa'n't quite so still; she takes after her father's folks, all quiet and dutiful, and ain't got the least idea how to enjoy themselves; we was all kind of noisy to our house when I was grown up, and I can't seem to sense the Deems."

"I often wish I had just such a little girl as your Lucy," said Mrs. Parkins, with a sigh. She held her gray-and-black bonnet off with her left hand and looked at it without approval.

"I shall always continue to wear black for Mr. Parkins," she said, "but I had this piece of dark-gray ribbon and I thought I had better use it on my black felt; the felt is sort of rusty, now, and black silk trimmings increase the rusty appearance."

"They do so," frankly acknowledged Mrs. Deems. "Why don't you go an' get you a new one for meetin', Mrs. Parkins? Felts ain't high this season, an' you've got this for second wear."

"I've got one that's plenty good for best," replied Mrs. Parkins, without any change of expression. "It seems best to make this do one more winter." She began to rearrange the gray ribbon, and Mrs. Deems watched her with a twinkle in her eyes; she had something to say, and did not know exactly how to begin, and Mrs. Parkins knew it as well as she did, and was holding her back which made the occasion more and more difficult.

"There!" she exclaimed at last, boldly, "I expect you know what I've come to see you for, an' I can't set here and make talk no longer. May's well ask if you can do anything about the minister's present."

Mrs. Parkins' mouth was full of pins, and she removed them all, slowly, before she spoke. The sun went behind a low snow cloud along the horizon, and Mrs. Deems shone on alone. It was not very warm in the room, and she gathered her woolen shawl closer about her shoulders as if she were getting ready to go home.

"I don't know's I feel to give you anything today. Mrs. Deems," said Mrs. Parkins in a resolved tone. "I don't feel much acquainted with the minister's folks. I must say she takes a good deal upon herself; I don't like so much of a ma'am."

"She's one of the pleasantest, best women we ever had in town, I think," replied Mrs. Deems. "I was tellin' 'em the other day that I always felt as if she brought a pleasant feelin' wherever she came, so sisterly and own-folks-like. They've seen a sight o'trouble an must feel pinched at times, but she finds ways to do plenty o' kindnesses. I never see a mite of behavior in 'em as if we couldn't do enough for 'em because they was ministers. Some minister's folks has such expectin' ways, and the more you do the more you may; but it ain't so with the Lanes. They are always a thinkin' what they can do for other people, an' they do it, too. You never liked 'em, but I can't see why."

"He ain't the ablest preacher that ever was," said Mrs. Parkins.

"I don't care if he ain't; words is words, but a man that lives as Mr. Lane does, is the best o' ministers," answered Mrs. Deems.

"Well, I don't owe 'em nothin' today," said the hostess, looking up. "I haven't got it in mind to do for the minister's folks any more than I have; but I may send 'em some apples or somethin', by'n by."

"Jest as you feel," said Mrs. Deems, rising quickly and looking provoked. "I didn't know but what 'twould be a pleasure to you, same's 'tis to the rest of us."

"They ain't been here very long, and I pay my part to the salary, an' 'taint no use to overdo in such cases."

"They've been put to extra expense this fall, and have been very feeling and kind; real interested in all of us, and such a help to the parish as we ain't had for a good while before. Havin' to send their boy to the hospital has made it hard for 'em."

"Well, folks has to have their hard times, and minister's families can't escape. I am sorry about the boy, I'm sure," said Mrs. Parkins, generously. "Don't you go, Mrs. Deems; you ain't been to see me for a good while. I want you to see my bonnet in jest a minute."

"I've got to go way over to the Dilby's, and it's goin' to be dark early. I should be pleased to have you come an' see me. I've got to find Lucy and trudge along."

"I believe I won't rise to see you out o' the door, my lap's so full," said Mrs. Parkins politely, and so they parted. Lucy was hopping up and down by the front fence to keep herself warm and occupied.

"She didn't say anything about the butternuts, did she, Mother?" the child asked; and Mrs. Deems laughed and shook her head. Then they walked away down the road together, the big-mittened hand holding fast the little one, and the hooded heads bobbing toward each other now and then, as if they were holding a lively conversation. Mrs. Parkins looked after them two or three times, suspiciously at first, as if she thought they might be talking about her; then a little wistfully. She had come of a saving family and had married a saving man.

"Isn't Mrs. Parkins real poor, Mother?" little Lucy inquired in a compassionate voice.

Mrs. Deems smiled, and assured the child that there was nobody so well off in town except Colonel Drummond, so far as money went; but Mrs. Parkins took care neither to enjoy her means herself, nor to let anybody else. Lucy pondered this strange answer for awhile and then began to hop and skip along the rough road, still holding fast her mother's warm hand.

This was the twenty-first of December, and the day of the week was Monday. On Tuesday Mrs. Parkins did her frugal ironing, and on Wednesday she meant to go over to Haybury to put some money into the bank and to do a little shopping. Goods were cheaper in Haybury in some of the large stores, than they were at the corner store at home, and she had the horse and could always get dinner at her cousin's. To be sure, the cousin was always hinting for presents for herself or her children, but Mrs. Parkins could bear that, and always cleared her conscience by asking the boys over in haying time, though their help cost more than it came to with their growing appetites and the wear and tear of the house. Their mother came for a day's visit now and then, but everything at home depended upon her hardworking hands, as she had been early left a widow with little else to depend upon, until now, when the boys were out of school. One was doing well in the shoe factory and one in a store. Mrs. Parkins was really much attached to her cousin, but she thought if she once began to give, they would always be expecting something.

As has been said, Wednesday was the day set for the visit, but when Wednesday came it was a hard winter day, cold and windy, with an occasional flurry of snow and, Mrs. Parkins being neuralgic, gave up going until Thursday. She was pleased when she waked Thursday morning to find the weather warmer and the wind stilled. She was weather-wise enough to see snow in the clouds, but it was only eight miles to Haybury and she could start early and come home again as soon as she got her dinner. So the boy who came every morning to take care of her horse and bring in wood was hurried and urged until he nearly lost his breath, and the horse was put into the wagon and, with rare forethought, a piece of salt pork was wrapped up and put under the wagon seat; then with a cloud over the re trimmed bonnet, and a shawl over her Sunday cloak, and mittens over her woolen gloves Mrs. Parkins drove away. All her neighbors knew that she was going to Haybury to put eighty-seven dollars into the bank that the Dilby brothers had paid her for some rye planted and harvested on the halves. Very likely she had a good deal of money beside, that day; she had the best farm in that sterile neighborhood and was a famous manager.

The cousin was a hospitable, kindly soul, very loyal to her relations and always ready with a welcome. Beside, though the ears of Lydia Parkins were deaf to hints of present need and desire, it was more than likely that she would leave her farm and savings to the boys; she was not a person to speak roughly to, or one whom it was possible to disdain. More than this, no truly compassionate heart could fail to pity the thin, anxious, forbidding little woman, who behaved as if she must always be on the defensive against a plundering and begging world.

Cousin Mary Faber, as usual, begged Mrs. Parkins to spend the night; she seemed to take so little pleasure in life that the change might do her good. There would be no expense except for the horse's stabling, Mrs. Faber urged openly, and nobody would be expecting her at home. But Mrs. Parkins as usual refused, and feared that the cellar would freeze. It had not been banked up as she liked to have it that autumn, but as for paying the Dilbys a dollar and a quarter for doing it, she didn't mean to please them so much.

"Land sakes! Why don't you feel as rich as you be, an' not mind them little expenses?" said Cousin Faber, daringly. "I do declare I don't see how you can make out to grow richer an' poorer at the same time." The good-natured soul could not help laughing as she spoke, and Mrs. Parkins herself really could not help smiling.

"I'm much obliged to you for the pleasure of your company," said Cousin Faber, and it was very considerate of you to bring me that nice piece o'pork." If she had only known what an effort her guest had made to carry it into the house after she had brought it! Twice Mrs. Parkins had pushed it back under the wagon seat with lingering indecision, and only taken it out at last because she feared that one of those prowling boys might discover it in the wagon and tell his mother. How often she had taken something into her hand to give away and then put it back and taken it again half a dozen times, irresolutely. There were still blind movements of the heart toward generosity, but she had grown more and more skillful at soothing her conscience and finding excuses for not giving.

The Christmas preparations in the busy little town made her uncomfortable, and cheerful Cousin Faber's happiness in her own pinched housekeeping was a rebuke. The boys' salaries were very small indeed, this first year or two; but their mother was proud of their steadiness, and still sewed and let rooms to lodgers and did everything she could to earn money. She looked tired and old before her time, and acknowledged to Mrs. Parkins that she should like to have a good, long visit at the farm the next summer and let the boys take their meals with a neighbor. "I never spared myself one step until they were through with their schooling; but now it will be so I can take things a little easier," said the good soul with a wistful tone that was unusual.

Mrs. Parkins felt impatient as she listened; she knew that a small present of money now and then would have been a great help, but she never could make up her mind to begin what promised to be the squandering of her carefully saved fortune. It would be the ruin of the boys, too, if they thought she could be appealed to in every emergency. She would make it up to them in the long run; she could not take her money with her to the next world, and she would make a virtue of necessity.

The afternoon was closing in cold and dark, and the snow came sifting down slowly before Mrs. Parkins was out of the street of Haybury. She had lived too long on a hill not to be weatherwise and for a moment, as the wind buffeted her face and she saw the sky and the horizon line all dulled by the coming storm, she had a great mind to go back to Cousin Faber's. If it had been any other time in the year but Christmas Eve! The old horse gathered his forces and hurried along as if he had sense enough to be anxious about the weather; but presently the road turned so that the wind was not so chilling and they were quickly out of sight of the town, crossing the level land which lay between Haybury and the hills of Holton. Mrs. Parkins was persuaded that she should get home by day, and the old horse did his very best. The road was rough and frozen and the wagon rattled and pitched along; it was like a race between Mrs. Parkins and the storm, and for a time it seemed certain that she would be the winner.

The gathering forces of the wind did not assert themselves fully until nearly half the eight miles had been passed, and the snow which had only clung to Mrs. Parkins' blanket-shawl like a white veil at first, and sifted white across the frozen grass of the lowlands, lay at last like a drift on the worn buffalo robe, and was so deep in the road that it began to clog the wheels. It was a most surprising snow in the thickness of the flakes and the rapidity with which it gathered; it was no use to try to keep the white knitted cloud over her face, for it became so thick with snow that it blinded and half-stifled her. The darkness began to fall, the snow came thicker and faster, and the horse climbing the drifted hills with the snow-clogged wagon, had to stop again and again. The awful thought suddenly came to Mrs. Parkins' mind that she could not reach home that night, and the next moment she had to acknowlege that she did not know exactly where she was. The thick flakes blinded her; she turned to look behind to see if anyone was coming; but she might have been in the middle of an Arctic waste. She felt benumbed and stupid, and again tried to urge the tired horse, and the good creature toiled on desperately. It seemed as if they must have left the lowland far enough behind to be near some houses, but it grew still darker and snowier as they dragged slowly for another mile until it was impossible to get any further, and the horse stopped still and then gave a shake to rid himself of the drift on his back, and turned his head to look inquiringly at his mistress.

Mrs. Parkins began to cry with cold, and fear and misery. She had read accounts of such terrible, sudden storms in the west, and here she was in the night, foodless, and shelterless, and helpless.

"Oh! I'd give a thousand dollars to be safe under cover!" groaned the poor soul. "Oh, how poor I be this minute, and I come right away from that warm house!"

A strange dazzle of light troubled her eyes, and a vision of the brightly lighted Haybury shops, and the merry customers that were hurrying in and out, and the gaiety and contagious generosity of Christmas Eve mocked at the stingy, little lost woman as she sat there half bewildered. The heavy flakes of snow caught her eyelashes and chilled her cheeks and melted inside the gray bonnet-strings; they heaped themselves on the top of the bonnet into a high crown that toppled into her lap as she moved. If she tried to brush the snow away, her clogged mitten only gathered more and grew more and more clumsy. It was a horrible, persistent storm; at this rate the horse and driver both would soon be covered and frozen in the road. The gathering flakes were malicious and mysterious; they were so large and flaked so fast down out of the sky.

"My goodness! How numb I be this minute," whispered Mrs.

Parkins. And then she remembered that the cashier of the bank had told her that morning when she made her deposit, that everybody else was taking out their money that day; she was the only one who had come to put any in.

"I'd pay every cent of it willin' to anybody that would come along and help me get to shelter," said the poor soul. "Oh, I don't know as I've hoed so's to be worth savin' "; and a miserable sense of shame and defeat beat down whatever hope tried to rise in her heart. What had she tried to do for God and man that gave her a right to think of love and succor now?

Yet it seemed every moment as if help must come and as if this great emergency could not be so serious. Life had been so monotonous to Mrs. Parkins, so destitute of excitement and tragic situations that she could hardly understand, even now, that she was in such great danger. Again she called as loud as she could for help, and the horse whinnied louder still. The only hope was that two men who had passed her some miles back would remember that they had advised her to hurry, and would come back to look for her. The poor old horse had dragged himself and the wagon to the side of the road under the shelter of some evergreens; Mrs. Parkins slipped down under the buffalo robe into the bottom of her cold old wagon, and covered herself as well as she could. There was more than a chance that she might be found frozen under a snowdrift in the morning.

The morning! Christmas morning!

What did the advent of Christmas day hold out for her—buried in the snowdrifts of a December storm!

Anything? Yes, but she knew it not. Little did she dream what this Christmas Eve was to bring into her life!

II

Lydia Parkins was a small woman of no great vigor, but as she grew a little warmer under her bed of blankets in the bottom of the old wagon, she came to her senses. She must get out and try to walk on through the snow as far as she could; it was no use to die there in this fearful storm like a rabbit. Yes, and she must unharness the horse and let him find his way; so she climbed boldly down into the knee-deep snow where a drift had blown already. She would not admit the thought that perhaps she might be lost in the snow and frozen to death that very night. It did not seem in character with Mrs. Nathan Parkins, who was the owner of plenty of money in Haybury Bank, and a good farm well-divided into tillage and woodland, who had plenty of blankets and comforters at home, and firewood enough, and suitable winter clothes to protect her from the weather. The wind was rising more and more, it made the wet gray-and-black bonnet feel very limp and cold about her head, and her poor head itself felt duller and heavier than ever. She lost one glove and mitten in the snow as she tried to unharness the old horse, and her bare fingers were very clumsy, but she managed to get the good old creature clear, hoping that he would plod on and be known farther along the road and get help for her; but instead of that he only went around and round her and the wagon, floundering and whinnying, and refusing to be driven away. "What kind of a storm is this going to be?" groaned Mrs. Parkins, wading along the road and falling over her dress helplessly. The old horse meekly followed and when she gave a weak, shrill, womanish shout, old Major neighed and shook the snow off his back. Mrs. Parkins knew in her inmost heart that, with such a wind and through such drifts, she could not get very far, and at last she lost her breath and sank down at the roadside and the horse went on alone. It was horribly dark and the cold pierced her through and through. In a few minutes she staggered to her feet and went on; she could have cried because the horse was out of sight, but she found it easier following in his tracks.

Suddenly there was a faint twinkle of light on the left, and what a welcome sight it was! The poor wayfarer hastened, but the wind behaved as if it were trying to blow her back. The horse had reached shelter first and somebody had heard him outside and came out and shut the house door with a loud bang that reached Mrs. Parkins' ears. She tried to shout again but she could hardly make a sound. The light still looked a good way off, but presently she could hear voices and see another light moving. She was so tired that she must wait until they came to help her. Who lived in the first house on the left after you passed Oak Ridge? Why, it couldn't be the Donnells, for they were all away in Haybury, and the house was shut up; this must be the parsonage, and she was off the straight road home. The bewildered horse had taken the left-hand road. "Well," thought Mrs. Parkins, "I'd rather be most anywhere else, but I don't care where 'tis so long as I get under cover. I'm all spent and wore out."

The lantern came bobbing along quickly as if somebody were hurrying, and wavered from side to side as if it were in a fishing boat on a rough sea. Mrs. Parkins started to meet it, and made herself known to her rescuer.

"I declare, if 'taint the minister," she exclaimed. "I'm Mrs. Parkins, or what's left of her. I've come near bein' froze to death along back here a-piece. I never saw such a storm in all my life."

She sank down in the snow and could not get to her feet again. The minister was a strong man, he stooped and lifted her like a child and carried her along the road with the lantern hung on his arm. She was a little woman and she was not a person given to sentiment, but she had been dreadfully cold and frightened, and now at last she was safe. It was like the good shepherd in the Bible, and Lydia Parkins was past crying; but it seemed as if she could never speak again and as if her heart were going to break. It seemed inevitable that the minister should have come to find her and carry her to the fold; no, to the parsonage; but she felt dizzy and strange again, and the second-best gray-and-black bonnet slipped its knot and tumbled off into the snow without her knowing it.

When Mrs. Parkins opened her eyes a bright light made them shut again directly; then she discovered, a moment afterward, that she was in the parsonage sitting room and the minister's wife was kneeling beside her with an anxious face; and there was a Christmas tree at the other side of the room, with all its pretty, shining things and gay little candles on the boughs. She was comfortably wrapped in warm blankets, but she felt very tired and weak. The minister's wife smiled with delight: "Now you'll feel all right in a few minutes," she exclaimed. "Think of your being out in this awful storm! Don't try to talk to us yet, dear," she added kindly. "I'm going to bring you a cup of good hot tea. Are you all right? Don't try to tell anything about the storm. Mr. Lane has seen to the horse. Here, I'll put my little red shawl over you, it looks prettier than the blankets, and I'm drying your clothes in the kitchen."

The minster's wife had a sweet face, and she stood for a minute looking down at her unexpected guest; then something in the thin, appealing face on the sofa seemed to touch her heart, and she stooped over and kissed Mrs. Parkins. It happened that nobody had kissed Mrs. Parkins for years, and the tears stole down her cheeks as Mrs. Lane turned away.

As for the minister's wife, she had often thought that Mrs. Parkins had a most disagreeable hard face; she liked her less than anyone in the parish, but now as she brightened the kitchen fire, she began to wonder what she could find to put on the Christmas tree for her, and wondered why she never had noticed a frightened, timid look in the poor woman's eyes. "It is so forlorn for her to live all alone on that big farm," said Mrs. Lane to herself, mindful of her own happy home and the children. All three of them came close about their mother at that moment, lame-footed John with his manly pale face, and smiling little Bell and Mary, the girls.

The minister came in from the barn and blew his lantern out and hung it away. The old horse was blanketed as warm as his mistress, and there was a good supper in his crib. It was a very happy household at the parsonage, and Mrs. Parkins could hear their whispers and smothered laughter in the kitchen. It was only eight o'clock after all, and it was evident that the children longed to begin their delayed festivities. The little girls came and stood in the doorway and looked first at the stranger guest and then at their Christmas tree, and after a while their mother came with them to ask whether Mrs. Parkins felt equal to looking on at the pleasuring or whether she would rather go to bed and rest, and sleep away her fatigue.

Mrs. Parkins wished to look on; she was beginning to feel well again, but she dreaded being alone, she could not tell exactly why.

"Come right into the bedroom with me then," said Mrs. Lane,

"and put on a nice warm, double gown of mine; 'twill be large enough for you that's certain, and then if you do wish to move about by-and-by, you will be better able than in the blankets."

Mrs. Parkins felt dazed by this little excitement, yet she was strangely in the mood for it. The reaction of being in this safe and pleasant place, after the recent cold and danger, excited her, and gave her an unwonted power of enjoyment and sympathy. She felt pleased and young, and she wondered what was going to happen. She stood still and let Mrs. Lane brush her gray hair, all tangled with the snow damp, as if she were no older than the little girls themselves; then they went out again to the sitting-room. There was a great fire blazing in the Franklin stove; the minister had cleared a rough bit of the parsonage land the summer before and shown good spirit about it, and these, as Mrs. Parkins saw at once, were some of the pitch-pine roots. She had said when she heard of his hard work, that he had better put the time into his sermons, and she remembered that now with a pang at her heart, and confessed inwardly that she had been mean spirited sometimes toward the Lanes, and it was a good lesson to her to be put at their mercy now. As she sat in her corner by the old sofa in the warm double gown and watched their kindly faces, a new sense of friendliness and hopefulness stole into her heart. "I'm just as warm now as I was cold a while ago," she assured the minister.

The children sat side by side, the lame boy and the two little sisters before the fire, and Mrs. Lane sat on the sofa by Mrs. Parkins, and the minister turned over the leaves of a Bible that lay on the table. It did not seem like a stiff and formal meeting held half from superstition and only half from reverence, but it was as if the good man were telling his household news of someone they all loved and held close to their hearts. He said a few words about the birth of Christ, and of there being no room that night in the inn. Room enough for the Roman soldier and the priest and the tax-gatherer, but no room for Christ; and how we all blame that innkeeper, and then are like him too often in the busy inn of our hearts. "Room for our friends and our pleasures and our gains, and no room for Christ," said the minister sadly, as the children looked soberly into the fire and tried to understand. Then they heard again the story of the shepherds and the star, and it was a more beautiful story than ever, and seemed quite new and wonderful; and then the minister prayed, and gave special thanks for the friend who made one of their household that night, because she had come through such great danger. Afterward the Lanes sang their Christmas hymn, standing about a little old organ which the mother played: "While shepherds watched their flocks by night—"

They sang it all together as if they loved the hymn, and when they stopped and the room was still again, Mrs. Parkins could hear the wind blow outside and the great elm branches sway and creak above the little house, and the snow clicked busily against the windows. There was a curious warmth at her heart; she did not feel frightened or lonely, or cold, or even selfish any more.

They lighted the candles on the Christmas tree, and the young people capered about and were brimming over with secrets and shouted with delight, and the tree shone and glistened brave in its gay trimming of walnuts covered with gold and silver paper, and little bags sewed with bright worsted, and all sorts of pretty home-made trifles. But when the real presents were discovered, the presents that meant no end of thought and management and secret self-denial, the brightest part of the household love and happiness shone out. One after another they came to bring Mrs. Parkins her share of the little tree's fruit until her lap was full as she sat on the sofa. One little girl brought a bag of candy, though there wasn't much candy on the tree; and the other gave her a bookmark, and the lame boy had a pretty geranium, grown by himself, with a flower on it, and came limping to put it in her hands; and Mrs. Lane brought a pretty hood that her sister had made for her a few weeks before, but her old one was still good and she did not need two. The minister had found a little book of hymns which a friend had given him at the autumn conference, and as Mrs. Parkins opened it, she happened to see these words: "Room to deny ourselves." She didn't know why the tears rushed to her eyes: "I've got to learn to deny myself of being mean," she thought, almost angrily. It was the least she could do, to do something friendly for these kind people;

they had taken her in out of the storm with such loving warmth of sympathy; they did not show the least consciousness that she had never spoken a kind word about them since they came to town; that she alone had held aloof when this dear boy, their only son, had fought through an illness which might leave him a cripple for life. She had heard that there was a hope of his being cured if by-and-by his father could carry him to New York to a famous surgeon there. But all the expense of the long journey and many weeks of treatment had seemed impossible. They were so thankful to have him still alive and with them that Christmas night. Mrs. Parkins could see the mother's eyes shine with tears as she looked at him, and the father put out a loving hand to steady him as he limped across the room.

"I wish little Lucy Deems, that lives next neighbor to me, was here to help your girls keep Christmas," said Mrs. Parkins, speaking half-unconsciously. "Her mother has had it very hard; I mean to bring her over some day when the traveling gets good."

"We know Lucy Deems," said the children with satisfaction. Then Mrs. Parkins thought with regret of Cousin Faber and her two boys, and was sorry that they were not all at the minister's too. She seemed to have entered upon a new life; she even thought of her dreary home with disapproval, and of its comfortable provisioning in cellar and garret, and of her money in the Haybury bank, with secret shame. Here she was with Mrs. Lane's double gown on, as poor a woman as there was in the world; she had come like a beggar to the Lanes' door that Christmas Eve, and they were eagerly giving her houseroom and gifts great and small; where were her independence and her riches now? She was a stranger and they had taken her in, and they did it for Christ's sake, and he would bless them, but what was there to say for herself? "Lord, how poor I be!" faltered Lydia Parkins for the second time that night.

There had not been such a storm for years. It was days before people could hear from each other along the blockaded country roads. Men were frozen to death, and cattle; and the telegraph wires were down and the safe and comfortable countryside felt as if it had been in the power of some merciless and furious force of nature from which it could never again feel secure. But the sun came out and the blue jays came back, and the crows, and the white snow melted, and the farmers went to and fro again along the highways. A new peace and goodwill showed itself between the neighbors after their separation, but Mrs. Parkins' goodwill outshone the rest. She went to Haybury as soon as the roads were well broken, and brought Cousin Faber back with her for a visit, and sent her home again with a loaded wagon of supplies. She called in Lucy Deems and gave her a peck basketful of butternuts on New Year's Day, and told her to come for more when these were gone; and, more than all, one Sunday soon afterward, the minister told his people that he should be away for the next two Sundays. The kindness of a friend was going to put a great blessing within his reach, and he added simply, in a faltering voice, that he hoped all his friends would pray for the restoration to health of his dear boy.

Mrs. Parkins sat in her pew; she had not worn so grim an expression since before Christmas. Nobody could tell what secret pangs these gifts and others like them had cost her, yet she knew that only a right way of living would give her peace of mind. She could no longer live in a mean, narrow world of her own making; she must try to take the world as it is, and make the most of her life.

There were those who laughed and said that her stingy ways were frightened out of her on the night of the storm; but sometimes one is taught and led slowly to a higher level of existence unconsciously and irresistibly, and the decisive upward step once taken is seldom retraced. It was not long before Mrs. Deems said to a neighbor cheerfully: "Why, I always knew Mrs. Parkins meant well enough, but she didn't know how to do for other folks; she seemed kind of scared to use her own money, as if she didn't have any right to it. Now she is kind of persuaded that she's got the whole responsibility, and just you see how pleased she behaves. She's just a beginnin' to live; she never heard one word o' the first prayer yesterday mornin'; I see her beamin' an' smilin' at the minster's boy from the minute she see him walk up the aisle straight an' well as anybody."

"She goin' to have one of her Cousin Faber's sons come over and stop awhile, I hear. He got run down workin' in the shoe factory to Haybury. Perhaps he may take hold and she'll let him take the farm by-an'-by. There, we mustn't expect too much of her," said the other woman compassionately. "I'm sure 'tis a blessed change as far as she's got a'ready. Habits'll live sometimes after they're dead. Folks don't find it so easy to go free of ways they've settled into; life's truly a warfare, ain't it?"

"It is so," answered Mrs. Deems, soberly. "There comes Mrs. Parkins this minute, in the old wagon, and my Lucy settin' up 'long side of her as pert as Nathan! Now ain't Mrs. Parkins' countenance got a pleasanter look than it used to wear? Well, the more she does for others, and the poorer she gets, the richer she seems to feel."

"It's a very unusual circumstance for a woman o' her age to turn right about in her tracks. It makes us believe that Heaven takes hold and helps folks," said the neighbor; and they watched the thin, little woman out of sight along the hilly road with a look of pleased wonder on their own faces. It was midspring, but Mrs. Parkins still wore her best winter bonnet; as for the old rusty one trimmed with gray, the minster's little girls found it when the snowdrifts melted, and carefully hid it away to deck the parsonage scarecrow in the time of corn planting.

The Legend of Saint Nicholas

GEORGENE FAULKNER

ONCE UPON A TIME there lived in Myra a good man named Nicholas. When he was a young man his father and mother died of the plague, and he was left the sole heir of all their vast estate. But he looked upon all this money as belonging to God and felt that he, himself, was merely the steward of God's mercies. So he went about everywhere doing good and sharing his riches with all those who were in need.

Now, there lived in that country a certain nobleman who had three beautiful daughters. He had been very rich, but he lost all his property and became so poor that he did not know what to do to provide for his family. His daughters were anxious to be married, but their father had no money to give them dowries and, in that country, no maiden could marry unless she had her marriage portion, or dowry. They were so very poor that they had scarcely enough food to eat. Their clothes were so worn and ragged that they would not go out of the house and their father was overcome with shame and sorrow.

When the good Nicholas heard of their troubles he longed to help them. He knew that the father was proud and that it would be hard to give him money; so he thought that it would be best to surprise them with a gift. Then Nicholas took some gold and, tying it in a long silken purse, went at once to the home of the poor nobleman. It was night and the beautiful maidens were fast asleep while the broken-hearted father, too wretched to go to bed, sat by the fireside watching and praying.

Nicholas stood outside, wondering how he could bestow his gift without being seen, when suddenly the moon came from behind the clouds and he saw that a window in the house was open. Creeping softly to the open window, he threw the purse right into

the room where it fell at the feet of the nobleman. The father picked up the purse and was very surprised to find it full of gold pieces.

Awakening his daughters the father said, "See this purse which came through the window and fell at my feet. It is indeed a gift from Heaven. God has remembered us in our time of need."

After they had rejoiced together, they agreed to give most of the gold to the eldest daughter, so that she would have her dowry and could wed the young man she loved.

Not long after that, Nicholas filled another silken purse with gold and again he went by night so that no one should see him, and he threw this purse, too, through the open window. When the father saw this golden gift he again gave thanks. The money he gave to the second daughter who, like her sister, at once married the man of her choice.

Meanwhile the father was curious to find out who was so kind to them, for he wished to thank the person who had come in the night to help them with these golden gifts. So he watched and waited night after night. And after a time the good Nicholas came with another silken purse filled with gold pieces for the youngest daughter.

He was just about to throw it into the room when the nobleman rushed from the house and, seizing him by his long robe, knelt before him, saying, "Oh good Nicholas, servant of God, why seek to hide thyself?" And he kissed his hands and feet and tried to thank him.

But Nicholas answered, "Do not thank me, my good man, but thank the Heavenly Father who has sent me to you in answer to your prayers. I am only His messenger to help those who trust in Him. Tell no man of these gifts of gold, nor who brought them to you in the night, for my deeds are done in His name."

Thus the youngest daughter of the nobleman was married, and she and her father and sisters all lived happily the rest of their lives.

The good Nicholas went about from place to place, and wherever he went he did deeds of kindness, so that all the people loved him.

One time he took a long journey to the Holy Land, and when he was upon the sea there came a terrible storm, so that the ship was tossed about and almost wrecked, and all the sailors gave up hope.

But the good Nicholas said, "Fear not, our Heavenly Father will bring us safely into harbor." Then he knelt and prayed to God and the storm ceased and the boat was brought safely to the land. Whereupon the sailors fell at the feet of Nicholas and thanked him.

He answered them humbly, "Thank your Father who is in

Heaven, for He is the ruler of us all. It is He who rules the earth and the sky and the sea, and who, in His good mercy, spared our lives that we may serve Him."

When Nicholas returned from Palestine he went to the city of Myra, where he was appointed a bishop. After that he preached God's Word and went about doing good all of his life. When he died the people said, "We will not call him Bishop Nicholas, but we will call him Saint Nicholas, for if ever there was a saint upon earth it was our good Nicholas." And so to this day he is called Good Saint Nicholas.

And now in many countries they tell the story of the good Saint Nicholas, and how he goes about the earth at Christmas time bringing gifts of love to all who deserve them, and, because he had put his gifts of gold in long silken purses, today children hang up their long stockings to hold his gifts. And when the children are very good he fills their stockings with sweets and toys and trinkets, but if they have been naughty, they will find a bunch of switches, showing that they deserve to be punished.

We all know that on Christmas Eve Saint Nicholas will come in the night, for he never likes to be seen. And we know that he will always live—for he is the spirit of love and love can never die.

So, every Christmas, let us give our gifts as he did those silken purses so long ago—without anyone knowing about it—and let our gifts be a surprise. Then we, too, can have the spirit of love and join in this celebration of Christmas with good Saint Nicholas.

The Fir Tree

HANS CHRISTIAN ANDERSEN

OUT IN THE WOODS stood a nice little fir tree. The place he had was a very good one; the sun shone on him; as to fresh air, there was enough of that, and round him grew many large-sized comrades, pines as well as firs. But the little fir wanted so very much to be a grown-up tree.

He did not think of the warm sun and of the fresh air; he did not care for the little children who ran about and prattled when they were in the woods looking for wild strawberries. The children often came with a whole pitcherful of berries, or a long row of them threaded on a straw, and sat down near the young tree and said, "Oh, how pretty he is! What a nice little fir!" But this was what the tree could not bear to hear.

At the end of a year he had shot up a good deal, and after another year he was another long bit taller; for with fir trees one can always tell by the shoots how many years old they are.

"Oh, were I but such a high tree as the others are!" sighed he. "Then I should be able to spread out my branches and with the tops look into the wide world! Then would the birds build nests among my branches; and when there was a breeze I could bend with as much stateliness as the others!"

Neither the sunbeams, nor the birds, nor the red clouds which morning and evening sailed above him gave the little tree any pleasure.

In winter, when the snow lay glittering on the ground, a hare would often come leaping along and jump right over the little tree. Oh, that made him so angry! But two winters were past, and in the third the tree was so large that the hare was obliged to go around it. To grow and grow, to get older and be tall, thought the tree—that, after all, is the most delightful thing in the world!

In autumn the woodcutters always came and felled some of the largest trees. This happened every year; and the young fir tree, that had now grown to a very comely size, trembled at the sight; for the magnificent great trees fell to the earth with noise and cracking, the branches were lopped off, and the trees looked long and bare; they were hardly to be recognized; and then they were laid in carts, and the horses dragged them out of the wood.

Where did they go to? What became of them?

In spring, when the swallows and the storks came, the tree asked them, "Don't you know where they have been taken? Have you not met them anywhere?"

The swallows did not know anything about it. But the stork looked musing, nodded his head, and said, "Yes, I think I know. I met many ships as I was flying hither from Egypt; on the ships were magnificent masts, and I venture to assert that it was they that smelled so of fir. I may congratulate you, for they lifted themselves on high most majestically!"

"Oh, were I but old enough to fly across the sea! But how does the sea look in reality? What is it like?"

"That would take a long time to explain," said the stork; and with these words off he went.

"Rejoice in thy growth!" said the sunbeams. "Rejoice in thy vigorous growth and in the fresh life that moveth within thee!"

And the wind kissed the tree, and the dew wept tears over him; but the fir understood it not.

When Christmas came, quite young trees were cut down, trees which often were not even as large or of the same age as this fir tree who could never rest but always wanted to be off. These young trees, and they were always the finest-looking, retained their branches. They were laid on carts, and the horses drew them out of the wood.

"Where are they going to?" asked the fir. "They are not taller than I; there was one indeed that was considerably shorter—and why do they retain all their branches? Whither are they taken?"

"We know! We know!" chirped the sparrows. "We have peeped in at the windows in the town below! We know where they are taken! The greatest splendor and the greatest magnificence one can imagine await them. We peeped through the windows and saw them planted in the middle of the warm room, and ornamented with the most splendid things—with gilded apples, with gingerbread, with toys and many hundred lights!"

"And then?" asked the fir tree, trembling in every bough. "And then? What happens then?"

"We did not see anything more; it was incomparably beautiful."

"I would be happy to know that I am destined for so glorious a career," cried the tree, rejoicing. "That is still better than to cross the sea! What a longing do I suffer! Were Christmas but come! I am now tall, and my branches spread like the others that were carried off last year! Oh, were I but already on the cart! Were I in the warm room with all the splendor and magnificence! Yes; then something better, something still grander, will surely follow, or why else should they thus ornament me? Something better, something still grander, *must* follow—but what? Oh, how I long, how I suffer! I do not know myself what is the matter with me!"

"Rejoice in our presence!" said the air and the sunlight; "Rejoice in thy own fresh youth!"

But the tree did not rejoice at all. He grew and grew, and was green both winter and summer. People that saw him said, "What a fine tree!" and toward Christmas he was one of the first that was cut down. The ax struck deep into the very pith. The tree fell to the earth with a sigh. He felt a pang—it was like a swoon. He could not think of happiness, for he was sorrowful at being separated from his home, from the place where he had sprung up. He well knew that he should never see his dear old comrades, the little bushes and flowers around him, anymore, perhaps not even the birds! The departure was not at all agreeable.

The tree only came to himself when he was unloaded in a court-yard with the other trees, and heard a man say, "That one is splen-did; we don't want the others." Then two servants came in rich liv-ery and carried the fir tree into a large and splendid drawing room. Portraits were hanging on the walls, and near the white porcelain stove stood two large Chinese vases with lions on the covers. There, too, were large easy chairs, silken sofas, large tables full of picture books and full of toys worth hundreds and hundreds of crowns—at least the children said so. And the fir tree was stuck upright in a cask that was filled with sand. But no one could see that it was a cask, for green cloth was hung all around it, and it stood on a large, gaily colored carpet. Oh, how the tree quivered! What was to happen?

The servants as well as the young ladies decorated it. On one branch there hung little nets cut out of colored paper, and each net was filled with sugarplums; and among the other boughs gilded apples and walnuts were suspended, looking as though they had grown there, and little blue and white candles were placed among the leaves. Dolls that looked for all the world like men—the tree had never beheld such before—were seen among the foliage, and at the very top a large star of gold tinsel was fixed. It was really splendid— beyond description splendid.

"This evening!" said they all. "How it will shine this evening!"

Oh, thought the tree, if the evening were but come! If the candles were but lighted! And then I wonder what will happen! Perhaps the other trees from the forest will come to look at me! Perhaps the sparrows will beat against the windowpanes! I wonder if I shall take root here and winter and summer stand covered with ornaments!"

He knew very much about the matter! But he was so impatient that for sheer longing he got a pain in his back, and this with trees is the same thing as a headache with us.

The candles were now lighted. What brightness! What splendor! The tree trembled so in every bough that one of the candles set fire to the foliage. It blazed up splendidly.

"Help! help!" cried the young ladies, and they quickly put out the fire.

Now the tree did not even dare tremble. What a state he was in! He was so uneasy lest he should lose something of his splendor that he was quite bewildered amid the glare and brightness, when suddenly both folding doors opened and a troop of children rushed in as if they would upset the tree. The older persons followed quietly. The little ones stood quite still. But it was only for a moment; then they shouted so that the whole place reechoed with their rejoicing. They danced around the tree, and one present after the other was pulled off.

What are they about? thought the tree. What is to happen now? And the lights burned down to the very branches, and as they burned down they were put out one after the other, and then the children had permission to plunder the tree. So they fell upon it with such violence that all its branches cracked. If it had not been fixed firmly in the cask it would certainly have tumbled down.

The children danced about with their beautiful playthings. No one looked at the tree except the old nurse, who peeped between the branches; but it was only to see if there was a fig or an apple left that had been forgotten.

"A story! A story!" cried the children, drawing a little fat man toward the tree. He seated himself under it and said, "Now we are in the shade, and the tree can listen too. But I shall tell only one story.

Now which will you have: that about Ivedy-Avedy, or about Klumpy-Dumpy who tumbled downstairs, and yet after all came to the throne and married the princess?"

"Ivedy-Avedy," cried some; "Klumpy-Dumpy," cried the others. There was such a bawling and screaming. The fir tree alone was silent, and he thought to himself, Am I not to bawl with the rest— am I to do nothing whatever? For he was one of the company and had done what he had to do.

And the man told about Klumpy-Dumpy that tumbled down, who notwithstanding came to the throne and at last married the princess. And the children clapped their hands and cried out, "Oh, go on! Do go on!" They wanted to hear about Ivedy-Avedy, too, but the little man only told them about Klumpy-Dumpy. The fir tree stood quite still and absorbed in thought; the birds in the wood had never related the like of this. Klumpy-Dumpy fell downstairs, and yet he married the princess! Yes, yes! That's the way of the world! thought the fir tree, and believed it all, because the man who told the story was so good-looking. Well, well! Who knows, perhaps I may fall downstairs, too, and get a princess as wife! And he looked forward with joy to the morrow, when he hoped to be decked out again with lights, playthings, fruits, and tinsel.

I won't tremble tomorrow! thought the fir tree. I will enjoy to the full all my splendor! Tomorrow I shall hear again the story of Klumpy-Dumpy, and perhaps that of Ivedy-Avedy, too. And the whole night the tree stood still and in deep thought.

In the morning the servant and the housemaid came in.

Now, then, the splendor will begin again, thought the fir. But they dragged him out of the room, and up the stairs into the loft; and here in a dark corner, where no daylight could enter, they left him. What's the meaning of this? thought the tree. What am I to do here? What shall I hear now, I wonder? And he leaned against the wall, lost in reverie. Time enough had he, too, for his reflections, for days and nights passed on, and nobody came up; and when at last somebody did come it was only to put some great trunks in a corner out of the way. There stood the tree, quite hidden; it seemed as if he had been entirely forgotten.

'Tis now winter out-of-doors! thought the tree. The earth is hard and covered with snow. Men cannot plant me now, and therefore I have been put up here under shelter till the springtime comes! How thoughtful that is! How kind man is, after all! If it only were not so dark here and so terribly lonely! Not even a hare. And out in the woods it was so pleasant when the snow was on the ground, and the hare leaped by; yes, even when he jumped over me; but I did not like it then. It is really terribly lonely here!"

"Squeak! Squeak!" said a little mouse, at the same moment peeping out of his hole. And then another little one came.

They snuffed about the fir tree and rustled among the branches.

"It is dreadfully cold," said the mouse. "But for that it would be delightful here, old fir, wouldn't it?"

"I am by no means old," said the fir tree. "There's many a one considerably older than I am."

"Where do you come from," asked the mice, "and what can you do?" They were so extremely curious. "Tell us about the most beautiful spot on the earth. Have you never been there? Were you never in the larder where cheeses lie on the shelves and hams hang from above, where one dances about on tallow candles; that place where one enters lean and comes out again fat and portly?"

"I know no such place," said the tree. "But I know the wood, where the sun shines, and where the little birds sing." And then he told all about his youth; and the little mice had never heard the like before; and they listened and said, "Well, to be sure! How much you have seen! How happy you must have been!"

"I?" said the fir tree, thinking over what he had himself related. "Yes, in reality those were happy times." And then he told about Christmas Eve, when he was decked out with cakes and candles.

"Oh," said the little mice, "how fortunate you have been, old fir tree!"

"I am by no means old," said he. "I came from the wood this winter; I am in my prime, and am only rather short for my age."

"What delightful stories you know!" said the mice; and the next night they came with four other little mice, who were to hear what the tree recounted. And the more he related the more plainly he remembered all himself; and it appeared as if those times had really been happy times. "But they may still come—they may still come. Klumpy-Dumpy fell downstairs, and yet he got a princess!" And he thought at the moment of a nice little birch tree growing out in the wood. To the fir that would be a real charming princess.

"Who is Klumpy-Dumpy?" asked the mice. So then the fir tree told the whole fairy tale, for he could remember every single word of it; and the little mice jumped for joy up to the very top of the tree. Next night two more mice came, and on Sunday two rats, even. But they said the stories were not interesting, which vexed the little mice; and they, too, now began to think them not so very amusing, either.

"Do you know only one story?" asked the rats.

"Only that one," answered the tree. "I heard it on my happiest evening; but I did not then know how happy I was."

"It is a very stupid story! Don't you know one about bacon and tallow candles? Can't you tell any larder stories?"

"No," said the tree.

"Then good-bye," said the rats; and they went home.

At last the little mice stayed away too, and the tree sighed. "After all, it was very pleasant when the sleek little mice sat round me and listened to what I told them. Now that, too, is over. But I will take good care to enjoy myself when I am brought out again."

But when was that to be? Why, one morning there came a quantity of people who set to work in the loft. The trunks were moved, the tree was pulled out and thrown—rather hard, it is true—down on the floor, but a man drew him toward the stairs, where the daylight shone.

Now a merry life will begin again, thought the tree. He felt the fresh air, the first sunbeam—and now he was out in the courtyard. All passed so quickly, there was so much going on around him, that the tree quite forgot to look to himself. The court adjoined a garden, and all was in flower. The roses hung so fresh and odorous over the balustrade, the lindens were in blossom, the swallows flew by and said, "Quirre-vit! My husband is come!" but it was not the fir tree that they meant.

"Now, then, I shall really enjoy life," said he, exultingly, and spread out his branches. But, alas! they were all withered and yellow. It was in a corner that he lay, among weeds and nettles. The golden star of tinsel was still on the top of the tree, and glittered in the sunshine.

In the courtyard some of the merry children were playing who had danced at Christmas round the fir tree and were so glad at the sight of him. One of the youngest ran and tore off the golden star.

"Only look what is still on the ugly old Christmas tree!" said he, trampling on the branches so that they all cracked beneath his feet.

And the tree beheld all the beauty of the flowers and the freshness in the garden; he beheld himself and wished he had remained in his dark corner in the loft. He thought of his first youth in the wood, of the merry Christmas Eve, and of the little mice who had listened with so much pleasure to the story of Klumpy-Dumpy.

"'Tis over! 'Tis past!" said the poor tree. "Had I but rejoiced when I had reason to do so! But now 'tis past, 'tis past!"

And the gardener's boy chopped the tree into small pieces; there was a whole heap lying there. The wood flamed up splendidly under the large brewing cauldron, and it sighed so deeply! Each sigh was like a shot.

The boys played about in the court, and the youngest wore on his breast the gold star which the tree had had on the happiest evening of his life. However, that was over now—the tree gone, the story at an end. All, all was over. Every tale must end at last.

Is There a Santa Claus?

IN SEPTEMBER 1871 eight-year-old Virginia Hanlon of West 95th Street in New York City wrote the following letter to *The New York Sun:*

> Dear Editor,
>
> *I am eight years old. Some of my friends say there is no Santa Claus. Papa says, "If you see it in the* Sun, *it's so." Please tell me the truth, Is there a Santa Claus?*

In one of the most famous editorials ever written, the editors replied:

Virginia, your little friends are wrong. They have been affected by the skepticism of a skeptical age. They do not believe except what they see. They think that nothing can be which is not comprehensible by their little minds. All minds, Virginia, whether they be men's or children's, are little. In this great universe of ours man is a mere insect, an ant, in his intellect, as compared with the boundless world about him, as measured by the intelligence capable of grasping the whole of truth and knowledge.

Yes, Virginia, there is a Santa Claus. He exists as certainly as love and generosity and devotion exist, and you know that they abound and give to your life its highest beauty and joy. Alas! how dreary would be the world if there were no Santa Claus! It would be as dreary as if there were no Virginias. There would be no childlike faith, no poetry, no romance to make tolerable this existence. We should have no enjoyment, except in sense and sight. The eternal light with which childhood fills the world would be extinguished.

Not believe in Santa Claus! You might as well not believe in fairies! You might get your papa to hire men to watch in all the chimneys on Christmas eve to catch Santa Claus, but even if they did not see Santa Claus come down, what would that prove? Nobody sees Santa Claus, but that is no sign that there is no Santa Claus. The most real things in the world are those that neither children nor men can see. Did you ever see fairies dancing on the lawn? Of course not, but that's no proof that they are not there. Nobody can conceive or imagine all the wonders there are unseen and unseeable in the world.

You tear apart the baby's rattle and see what makes the noise inside, but there is a veil covering the unseen world which not the strongest man, nor even the united strength of all the strongest men that ever lived, could tear apart. Only faith, fancy, poetry, love, romance, can push aside that curtain and view and picture the supernal beauty and glory beyond. Is it all real? Ah, Virginia, in all this world there is nothing else real and abiding.

No Santa Claus! Thank God he lives, and he lives forever. A thousand years from now, Virginia, nay, ten times ten thousand years from now, he will continue to make glad the heart of childhood.

Christmas Thoughts

WASHINGTON IRVING

O F ALL THE OLD FESTIVALS, that of Christmas awakens the strong-est and most heartfelt associations. There is a tone of solemn and sacred feeling that blends with our conviviality and lifts the spirit to a state of hallowed and elevated enjoyment.

It is a beautiful arrangement, derived from days of yore, that this festival, which commemorates the announcement of the religion of peace and love, has been made the season for gathering together of family connections, and drawing closer again those bands of kin-dred hearts which the cares, and pleasures, and sorrows of the world are continually operating to cast loose; of calling back the children of a family, who have launched forth in life, once more to assemble about the paternal hearth, there to grow young and loving again among the endearing mementos of childhood.

There is something in the very season of the year that gives a charm to the festivity of Christmas. In the depth of winter, when Nature lies despoiled of her charms, wrapped in her shroud of sheeted snow, we turn for our gratifications to moral sources. Heart calleth unto heart, and we draw our pleasures from the deep wells of loving kindness which lie in the quiet recesses of our bosoms.

Amidst the general call to happiness, the bustle of the spirits and stir of the affections, which prevail at this period, what bosom can remain insensible? It is indeed the season of regenerated feeling—the season for kindling not merely the fire of hospitality in the hall, but the genial flame of charity in the heart. He who can turn churl-ishly away from contemplating the felicity of his fellow-beings and can sit down repining in loneliness, when all around is joyful, wants the genial and social sympathies which constitute the charm of a merry Christmas.

A March Christmas

LOUISA MAY ALCOTT

"CHRISTMAS WON'T BE CHRISTMAS without any presents," grumbled Jo, lying on the rug.

"It's so dreadful to be poor!" sighed Meg, looking down at her old dress.

"I don't think it's fair for some girls to have plenty of pretty things, and other girls nothing at all," added little Amy, with an injured sniff.

"We've got Father and Mother and each other," said Beth contentedly, from her corner.

The four young faces on which the firelight shone brightened at the cheerful words, but darkened again as Jo said sadly, "We haven't got Father, and shall not have him for a long time." She didn't say "perhaps never," but each silently added it, thinking of Father far away, where the fighting was.

Nobody spoke for a minute; then Meg said in an altered tone, "You know the reason Mother proposed not having any presents this Christmas was because it is going to be a hard winter for everyone; and she thinks we ought not to spend money for pleasure, when our men are suffering so in the army. We can't do much, but we can make our little sacrifices, and ought to do it gladly. But I am afraid I don't"; and Meg shook her head, as she thought regretfully of all the pretty things she wanted.

"But I don't think the little we should spend would do any good. We've each got a dollar, and the army wouldn't be much helped by our giving that. I agree not to expect anything from Mother or you, but I do want to buy *Undine and Sintram* for myself; I've wanted it *so* long," said Jo, who was a bookworm.

"I planned to spend mine on new music," said Beth, with a little sigh, which no one heard but the hearth-brush and kettle-holder.

"I shall get a nice box of Faber's drawing pencils; I really need them," said Amy decidedly.

"Mother didn't say anything about our money, and she won't wish us to give up everything. Let's each buy what we want, and have a little fun; I'm sure we work hard enough to earn it," cried Jo, examining the heels of her shoes in a gentlemanly manner.

"I know *I* do—teaching those tiresome children nearly all day, when I'm longing to enjoy myself at home," began Meg, in the complaining tone again.

"You don't have half such a hard time as I do," said Jo. "How would you like to be shut up for hours with a nervous, fussy old lady, who keeps you trotting, is never satisfied, and worries you till you're ready to fly out of the window or cry?"

"It's naughty to fret; but I do think washing dishes and keeping things tidy is the worst work in the world. It makes me cross; and my hands get so stiff, I can't practice well at all," and Beth looked at her rough hands with a sigh that anyone could hear that time.

"I don't believe any of you suffer as I do," cried Amy; "for you don't have to go to school with impertinent girls, who plague you if you don't know your lessons, and laugh at your dresses, and label your father if he isn't rich, and insult you when your nose isn't nice."

"If you mean *libel*, I'd say so, and not talk about *labels*, as if Papa was a pickle bottle," advised Jo, laughing.

"I know what I mean, and you needn't be *statirical* about it. It's proper to use good words, and improve your *vocabilary*," returned Amy, with dignity.

"Don't peck at one another, children. Don't you wish we had the money Papa lost when we were little, Jo? Dear me! how happy and good we'd be, if we had no worries!" said Meg, who could remember better times.

"You said the other day, you thought we were a deal happier than the King children, for they were fighting and fretting all the time, in spite of their money."

"So I did, Beth. Well, I think we are; for, though we do have to work, we make fun for ourselves, and are a pretty jolly set, as Jo would say."

"Jo does use such slang words!" observed Amy, with a reproving look at the long figure stretched on the rug. Jo immediately sat up, put her hands in her pockets, and began to whistle.

"Don't, Jo; it's so boyish!"

"That's why I do it."

"I detest rude, unladylike girls!"

"I hate affected, niminy-piminy chits!"

" 'Birds in their little nests agree,' " sang Beth, the peacemaker, with such a funny face that both sharp voices softened to a laugh, and the "pecking" ended for that time.

"Really, girls, you are both to be blamed," said Meg, beginning to lecture in her elder-sisterly fashion. "You are old enough to leave off boyish tricks, and to behave better, Josephine. It didn't matter so much when you were a little girl; but now you are so tall, and turn up your hair, you should remember that you are a young lady."

"I'm not! and if turning up my hair makes me one, I'll wear it in two tails till I'm twenty," cried Jo, pulling off her net, and shaking down a chestnut mane. "I hate to think I've got to grow up, and be Miss March, and wear long gowns, and look as prim as a China aster! It's bad enough to be a girl, anyway, when I like boys' games and work and manners! I can't get over my disappointment in not being a boy; and it's worse than ever now, for I'm dying to go and fight with Papa, and I can only stay at home and knit, like a poky old woman!" And Jo shook the blue army sock till the needles rattled like castanets, and her ball bounded across the room.

"Poor Jo! It's too bad, but it can't be helped; so you must try to be contented with making your name boyish, and playing brother to us girls," said Beth, stroking the rough head at her knee with a hand that all the dishwashing and dusting in the world could not make ungentle in its touch.

"As for you, Amy," continued Meg, "you are altogether too particular and prim. Your airs are funny now; but you'll grow up an affected little goose, if you don't take care. I like your nice manners and refined ways of speaking, when you don't try to be elegant; but your absurd words are as bad as Jo's slang."

"If Jo is a tomboy and Amy a goose, what am I, please?" asked Beth, ready to share the lecture.

"You're a dear, and nothing else," answered Meg warmly; and no one contradicted her, for the "Mouse" was the pet of the family.

As young readers like to know "how people look," we will take this moment to give them a little sketch of the four sisters, who sat knitting away in the twilight, while the December snow fell quietly without, and the fire crackled cheerfully within. It was a comfortable old room, though the carpet was faded and the furniture very plain; for a good picture or two hung on the walls, books filled the recesses, chrysanthemums and Christmas roses bloomed in the windows, and a pleasant atmosphere of home peace pervaded it.

Margaret, the eldest of the four, was sixteen, and very pretty, being plump and fair, with large eyes, plenty of soft, brown hair, a sweet mouth, and white hands, of which she was rather vain. Fifteen-year-old Jo was very tall, thin, and brown, and reminded one of a colt; for she never seemed to know what to do with her long limbs, which were very much in her way. She had a decided mouth, a comical nose, and sharp, gray eyes, which appeared to see everything, and were by turns fierce, funny, or thoughtful. Her long, thick hair was her one beauty; but it was usually bundled into a net, to be out of her way. Round shoulders had Jo, big hands and feet, a flyaway look to her clothes, and the uncomfortable appearance of a girl who was rapidly shooting up into a woman, and didn't like it. Elizabeth—or Beth, as everyone called her—was a rosy, smooth-haired, bright-eyed girl of thirteen, with a shy manner, a timid voice, and a peaceful expression, which was seldom disturbed. Her father called her "Little Tranquillity," and the name suited her excellently; for she seemed to live in a happy world of her own, only venturing out to meet the few whom she trusted and loved. Amy, though the youngest, was a most important person—in her own opinion at least. A regular snow maiden, with blue eyes, and yellow hair curling on her shoulders, pale and slender, and always carrying herself like a young lady mindful of her manners. What the characters of the four sisters were we will leave to be found out.

The clock struck six; and, having swept up the hearth, Beth put a pair of slippers down to warm. Somehow the sight of the old shoes had a good effect upon the girls; for Mother was coming, and everyone brightened to welcome her. Meg stopped lecturing, and lighted the lamp, Amy got out of the easy chair without being asked, and Jo forgot how tired she was as she sat up to hold the slippers nearer to the blaze.

"They are quite worn out; Marmee must have a new pair."

"I thought I'd get her some with my dollar," said Beth.

"No, I shall!" cried Amy.

"I'm the oldest," began Meg, but Jo cut in with a decided—"I'm the man of the family now Papa is away, and *I* shall provide the slippers, for he told me to take special care of Mother while he was gone."

"I'll tell you what we'll do," said Beth; "let's each get her something for Christmas, and not get anything for ourselves."

"That's like you, dear! What will we get?" exclaimed Jo.

Everyone thought soberly for a minute; then Meg announced, as if the idea was suggested by the sight of her own pretty hands, "I shall give her a nice pair of gloves."

"Army slippers, best to be had," cried Jo.

"Some handkerchiefs, all hemmed," said Beth.

"I'll get a little bottle of cologne; she likes it, and it won't cost much, so I'll have some left to buy my pencils," added Amy.

"How will we give the things?" asked Meg.

"Put them on the table, and bring her in and see her open the bundles. Don't you remember how we used to do on our birthdays?" answered Jo.

"I used to be so frightened when it was my turn to sit in the big chair with the crown on, and see you all come marching round to give the presents, with a kiss. I liked the things and the kisses, but it was dreadful to have you sit looking at me while I opened the bundles," said Beth, who was toasting her face and the bread for tea, at the same time.

"Let Marmee think we are getting things for ourselves, and then surprise her. We must go shopping tomorrow afternoon, Meg; there is so much to do about the play for Christmas night," said Jo, marching up and down, with her hands behind her back and her nose in the air.

"I don't mean to act any more after this time; I'm getting too old for such things," observed Meg, who was as much a child as ever about "dressing-up" frolics.

"You won't stop, I know, as long as you can trail round in a white gown with your hair down, and wear gold-paper jewelry. You are the best actress we've got, and there'll be an end of everything if you quit the boards," said Jo. "We ought to rehearse tonight. Come here, Amy, and do the fainting scene, for you are as stiff as a poker in that."

"I can't help it; I never saw anyone faint, and I don't choose to make myself all black and blue, tumbling flat as you do. If I can go down easily, I'll drop; if I can't, I shall fall into a chair and be graceful; I don't care if Hugo does come at me with a pistol," returned Amy, who was not gifted with dramatic power, but was chosen because she was small enough to be borne out shrieking by the villain of the piece.

"Do it this way; clasp your hands so, and stagger across the room, crying frantically, 'Roderigo! save me! save me!'" and away went Jo, with a melodramatic scream which was truly thrilling.

Amy followed, but she poked her hands out stiffly before her, and jerked herself along as if she went by machinery; and her "Ow!" was more suggestive of pins being run into her than of fear and anguish. Jo gave a despairing groan, and Meg laughed outright, while Beth let her bread burn as she watched the fun, with interest.

"It's no use! Do the best you can when the time comes, and if the audience laughs don't blame me. Come on, Meg."

Then things went smoothly, for Don Pedro defied the world in a speech of two pages without a single break; Hagar, the witch, chanted an awful incantation over her kettleful of simmering toads, with weird effect; Roderigo rent his chains asunder manfully, and Hugo died in agonies of remorse and arsenic, with a wild "Ha! ha!"

"It's the best we've had yet," said Meg, as the dead villain sat up and rubbed his elbows.

"I don't see how you can write and act such splendid things, Jo. You're a regular Shakespeare!" exclaimed Beth, who firmly believed that her sisters were gifted with wonderful genius in all things.

"Not quite," replied Jo modestly. "I do think 'The Witch's Curse, an Operatic Tragedy,' is rather a nice thing; but I'd like to try *Macbeth*, if we only had a trap door for Banquo. I always wanted to do the killing part. 'Is that a dagger that I see before me?' " muttered Jo, rolling her eyes and clutching at the air, as she had seen a famous tragedian do.

"No, it's the toasting fork, with mother's shoe on it instead of the bread. Beth's stagestruck!" cried Meg, and the rehearsal ended in a general burst of laughter.

"Glad to find you so merry, my girls," said a cherry voice at the door, and actors and audience turned to welcome a tall, motherly lady, with a "can-I-help-you" look about her which was truly delightful. She was not elegantly dressed, but a noble-looking woman, and the girls thought the gray cloak and unfashionable bonnet covered the most splendid mother in the world.

"Well, dearies, how have you got on today? There was so much to do, getting the boxes ready to go tomorrow, that I didn't come home to dinner. Has anyone called, Beth? How is your cold, Meg? Jo, you look tired to death. Come and kiss me, baby."

While making these maternal inquiries Mrs. March got her wet things off, her warm slippers on, and sitting down in the easy chair, drew Amy to her lap, preparing to enjoy the happiest hour of her busy day. The girls flew about, trying to make things comfortable, each in her own way. Meg arranged the tea table; Jo brought wood and set chairs, dropping, overturning, and clattering everything she touched; Beth trotted to and fro between parlor and kitchen, quiet and busy; while Amy gave directions to everyone, as she sat with her hands folded.

As they gathered about the table, Mrs. March said, with a particularly happy face, "I've got a treat for you after supper."

A quick, bright smile went round like a streak of sunshine. Beth clapped her hands, regardless of the biscuit she held, and Jo tossed up her napkin, crying, "A letter! a letter! Three cheers for Father!"

"Yes, a nice long letter. He is well, and thinks he shall get through the cold season better than we feared. He sends all sorts of loving wishes for Christmas, and an especial message to you girls," said

Mrs. March, patting her pocket as if she had got a treasure there.

"Hurry and get done! Don't stop to quirk your little finger, and simper over your plate, Amy," cried Jo, choking on her tea, and dropping her bread, butter side down, on the carpet, in her haste to get at the treat.

Beth ate no more, but crept away, to sit in her shadowy corner and brood over the delight to come, till the others were ready.

"I think it was so splendid of Father to go as a chaplain when he was too old to be drafted, and not strong enough for a soldier," said Meg warmly.

"Don't I wish I could go as a drummer, a *vivan*—what's its name? or a nurse, so I could be near him and help him," exclaimed Jo, with a groan.

"It must be very disagreeable to sleep in a tent, and eat all sorts of bad-tasting things, and drink out of a tin mug," sighed Amy.

"When will he come home, Marmee?" asked Beth, with a little quiver in her voice.

"Not for many months, dear, unless he is sick. He will stay and do his work faithfully as long as he can, and we won't ask for him back a minute sooner than he can be spared. Now come and hear the letter."

They all drew to the fire, Mother in the big chair with Beth at her feet, Meg and Amy perched on either arm of the chair, and Jo leaning on the back, where no one would see any sign of emotion if the letter should happen to be touching.

Very few letters were written in those hard times that were not touching, especially those which fathers sent home. In this one little was said of the hardships endured, the dangers faced, or the homesickness conquered; it was a cheerful, hopeful letter, full of lively descriptions of camp life, marches, and military news; and only at the end did the writer's heart overflow with fatherly love and longing for the little girls at home.

"Give them all my dear love and a kiss. Tell them I think of them by day, pray for them by night, and find my best comfort in their affection at all times. A year seems very long to wait before I see them, but remind them that while we wait we may all work, so

that these hard days need not be wasted. I know they will remember all I said to them, that they will be loving children to you, will do their duty faithfully, fight their bosom enemies bravely, and conquer themselves so beautifully, that when I come back to them I may be fonder and prouder than ever of my little women."

Everybody sniffed when they came to that part; Jo wasn't ashamed of the great tear that dropped off the end of her nose, and Amy never minded the rumpling of her curls as she hid her face on her mother's shoulder and sobbed out, "I *am* a selfish girl! but I'll truly try to be better, so he mayn't be disappointed in me by and by."

"We all will!" cried Meg. "I think too much of my looks, and hate to work, but won't any more, if I can help it."

"I'll try and be what he loves to call me, 'a little woman,' and not be rough and wild; but do my duty here instead of wanting to be somewhere else," said Jo, thinking that keeping her temper at home was a much harder task than facing a rebel or two down South.

Beth said nothing, but wiped away her tears with the blue army sock, and began to knit with all her might, losing no time in doing the duty that lay nearest her, while she resolved in her quiet little soul to be all that Father hoped to find her when the year brought round the happy coming home.

Mrs. March broke the silence that followed Jo's words, by saying in her cheery voice, "Do you remember how you used to play Pilgrim's Progress when you were little things? Nothing delighted you more than to have me tie my piece-bags on your backs for burdens, give you hats and sticks and rolls of paper, and let you travel through the house from the cellar, which was the City of Destruction, up, up, to the house top, where you had all the lovely things you could collect to make a Celestial City."

"What fun it was, especially going by the lions, fighting Apolylon, and passing through the Valley where the hobgoblins were!" said Jo.

"I liked the place where the bundles fell off and tumbled downstairs," said Meg.

"My favorite part was when we came out on the flat roof where our flowers and arbors and pretty things were, and all stood and sang for joy up there in the sunshine," said Beth, smiling, as if that pleasant moment had come back to her.

"I don't remember much about it, except that I was afraid of the cellar and the dark entry, and always liked the cake and milk we had up at the top. If I wasn't too old for such things, I'd rather like to play it over again," said Amy, who began to talk of renouncing childish things at the mature age of twelve.

"We never are too old for this, my dear, because it is a play we are playing all the time in one way or another. Our burdens are here, our road is before us, and the longing for goodness and happiness is the guide that leads us through many troubles and mistakes to the peace which is a true Celestial City. Now, my little pilgrims, suppose you begin again, not in play, but in earnest, and see how far on you can get before Father comes home."

"Really, Mother? Where are our bundles?" asked Amy, who was a very literal young lady.

"Each of you told what your burden was just now, except Beth; I rather think she hasn't got any," said her mother.

"Yes, I have; mine is dishes and dusters, and envying girls with nice pianos, and being afraid of people."

Beth's bundle was such a funny one that everybody wanted to laugh; but nobody did, for it would have hurt her feelings very much.

"Let us do it," said Meg thoughtfully. "It is only another name for trying to be good, and the story may help us; for though we do want to be good, it's hard work, and we forget, and don't do our best."

"We were in the Slough of Despond tonight, and Mother came and pulled us out as Help did in the book. We ought to have our roll of directions, like Christian. What shall we do about that?" asked Jo, delighted with the fancy which lent a little romance to the very dull task of doing her duty.

"Look under your pillows, Christmas morning, and you will find your guidebook," replied Mrs. March.

They talked over the new plan while old Hannah cleared the table; then out came the four little work baskets, and the needles flew as the girls made sheets for Aunt March. It was uninteresting sewing, but tonight no one grumbled. They adopted Jo's plan of dividing the long seams into four parts, and calling the quarters Europe, Asia, Africa, and America, and in that way got on capitally, especially when they talked about the different countries as they stitched their way through them.

At nine they stopped work, and sang, as usual, before they went to bed. No one but Beth could get much music out of the old piano; but she had a way of softly touching the yellow keys, and making a pleasant accompaniment to the simple songs they sang. Meg had a voice like a flute, and she and her mother led the little choir. Amy chirped like a cricket, and Jo wandered through the airs at her own sweet will, always coming out at the wrong place with a croak or a quaver that spoiled the most pensive tune. They had always done this from the time they could lisp "Crinkle, crinkle, 'ittle 'tar," and it had become a household custom, for the mother was a born singer. The first sound in the morning was her voice, as she went about the house singing like a lark; and the last sound at night was the same cheery sound, for the girls never grew too old for that familiar lullaby.

Jo was the first to wake in the gray dawn of Christmas morning. No stockings hung at the fireplace, and for a moment she felt as much disappointed as she did long ago, when her little sock fell down because it was so crammed with goodies. Then she remembered her mother's promise, and, slipping her hand under her pillow, drew out a little crimson-covered book. She knew it very well, for it was that beautiful old story of the best life ever lived, and Jo felt that it was a true guidebook for any pilgrim going the long journey. She woke Meg with a "Merry Christmas," and bade her see what was under her pillow. A green-covered book appeared, with the same picture inside, and a few words written by their mother, which made their one present very precious in their eyes. Presently Beth and Amy woke, to rummage and find their little books also, one dove-colored, the other blue; and all sat looking at and talking about them, while the east grew rosy with the coming day.

In spite of her small vanities, Margaret had a sweet and pious nature, which unconsciously influenced her sisters, especially Jo, who loved her very tenderly, and obeyed her because her advice was so gently given.

"Girls," said Meg seriously, looking from tumbled head beside her to the two little nightcapped ones in the room beyond, "Mother wants us to read and love and mind these books, and we must begin at once. We used to be faithful about it; but since Father went away, and all this war trouble unsettled us, we have neglected many things. You can do as you please; but *I* shall keep my book on the table here, and read a little every morning as soon as I wake, for I know it will do me good, and help me through the day."

Then she opened her new book and began to read. Jo put her arm round her, and, leaning cheek to cheek, read also, with the quiet expression so seldom seen on her restless face.

"How good Meg is! Come, Amy, let's do as they do. I'll help you with the hard words, and they'll explain things if we don't understand," whispered Beth, very much impressed by the pretty books and her sisters' example.

"I'm glad mine is blue," said Amy; and then the rooms were very still while the pages were softly turned, and the winter sunshine crept in to touch the bright heads and serious faces with a Christmas greeting.

"Where is Mother?" asked Meg, as she and Jo ran down to thank her for their gifts, half an hour later.

"Goodness only knows. Some poor creeter come a-beggin', and your ma went straight off to see what was needed. There never *was* such a woman for givin' away vittles and drink, clothes and firin'," replied Hannah, who had lived with the family since Meg was born, and was considered by them all more as a friend than a servant.

"She will be back soon, I think; so fry your cakes, and have everything ready," said Meg, looking over the presents which were collected in a basket and kept under the sofa, ready to be produced at the proper time. "Why, where is Amy's bottle of cologne?" she added, as the little flask did not appear.

"She took it out a minute ago, and went off with it to put a ribbon on it, or some such notion," replied Jo, dancing about the room to take the first stiffness off the new army slippers.

"How nice my handkerchiefs look, don't they? Hannah washed

and ironed them for me, and I marked them all myself," said Beth, looking proudly at the somewhat uneven letters which had cost her such labor.

"Bless the child! she's gone and put 'Mother' on them instead of 'M. March.' How funny!" cried Jo, taking up one.

"Isn't it right? I thought it was better to do it so, because Meg's initials are 'M.M.,' and I don't want anyone to use these but Marmee," said Beth, looking troubled.

"It's all right, dear, and a very pretty idea,—quite sensible, too, for no one can ever mistake now. It will please her very much, I know," said Meg, with a frown for Jo and a smile for Beth.

"There's Mother. Hide the basket, quick!" cried Jo, as a door slammed, and steps sounded in the hall.

Amy came in hastily, and looked rather abashed when she saw her sisters all waiting for her.

"Where have you been, and what are you hiding behind you?" asked Meg, surprised to see, by her hood and cloak, that lazy Amy had been out so early.

"Don't laugh at me, Jo! I didn't mean anyone should know till the time came. I only meant to change the little bottle for a big one, and I gave *all* my money to get it, and I'm truly trying not to be selfish any more."

As she spoke, Amy showed the handsome flask which replaced the cheap one; and looked so earnest and humble in her little effort to forget herself that Meg hugged her on the spot, and Jo pronounced her "a trump," while Beth ran to the window, and picked her finest rose to ornament the stately bottle.

"You see I felt ashamed of my present, after reading and talking about being good this morning, so I ran round the corner and changed it the minute I was up: and I'm *so* glad, for mine is the handsomest now."

Another bang of the street door sent the basket under the sofa, and the girls to the table, eager for breakfast.

"Merry Christmas, Marmee! Many of them! Thank you for our books; we read some, and mean to every day," they cried, in chorus.

"Merry Christmas, little daughters! I'm glad you began at once, and hope you will keep on. But I want to say one word before we sit down. Not far away from here lies a poor woman with a little newborn baby. Six children are huddled into one bed to keep from freezing, for they have no fire. There is nothing to eat over there; and the oldest boy came to tell me they were suffering hunger and cold. My girls, will you give them your breakfast as a Christmas present?"

They were all unusually hungry, having waited nearly an hour, and for a minute no one spoke; only a minute, for Jo exclaimed impetuously, "I'm so glad you came before we began!"

"May I go and help carry the things to the poor little children?" asked Beth, eagerly.

"*I* shall take the cream and the muffins," added Amy, heroically giving up the articles she most liked.

Meg was already covering the buckwheats, and piling the bread into one big plate.

"I thought you'd do it," said Mrs. March, smiling as if satisfied. "You shall all go and help me, and when we come back we will have bread and milk for breakfast, and make it up at dinner time."

They were soon ready, and the procession set out. Fortunately it was early, and they went through back streets, so few people saw them, and no one laughed at the queer party.

A poor, bare, miserable room it was, with broken windows, no fire, ragged bedclothes, a sick mother, wailing baby, and a group of pale, hungry children cuddled under one old quilt, trying to keep warm.

How the big eyes stared and the blue lips smiled as the girls went in!

"*Ach, mein Gott!* it is good angels come to us!" said the poor woman, crying for joy.

"Funny angels in hoods and mittens," said Jo, and set them laughing.

In a few minutes it really did seem as if kind spirits had been at work there. Hannah, who had carried wood, made a fire, and stopped up the broken panes with old hats and her own cloak. Mrs. March gave the mother tea and gruel, and comforted her with promises of help, while she dressed the little baby as tenderly as if it had been her own. The girls, meantime, spread the table, set the children round the fire, and fed them like so many hungry birds, laughing, talking, and trying to understand the funny broken English.

"*Das ist gut!*" "*Die Engel-kinder!*" cried the poor things, as they ate, and warmed their purple hands at the comfortable blaze.

The girls had never been called angel children before, and thought it very agreeable, especially Jo, who had been considered a "Sancho" ever since she was born. That was a very happy breakfast, though they didn't get any of it; and when they went away, leaving comfort behind, I think there were not in all the city four merrier people than the hungry girls who gave away their breakfast and contented themselves with bread and milk on Christmas morning.

"That's loving our neighbor better than ourselves, and I like it," said Meg, as they set out their presents, while their mother was upstairs collecting clothes for the poor Hummels.

Not a very splendid show, but there was a great deal of love done up in the few little bundles, and the tall vase of red roses, white chrysanthemums, and trailing vines, which stood in the middle, gave quite an elegant air to the table.

"She's coming! Strike up, Beth! Open the door, Amy! Three cheers for Marmee!" cried Jo, prancing about, while Meg went to conduct Mother to the seat of honor.

Beth played her gayest march, Amy threw open the door, and Meg enacted escort with great dignity. Mrs. March was both surprised and touched; and smiled with her eyes full as she examined her presents, and read the little notes which accompanied them. The slippers went on at once, a new handkerchief was slipped into her pocket, well scented with Amy's cologne, the rose was fastened in her bosom, and the nice gloves were pronounced a "perfect fit."

There was a good deal of laughing and kissing and explaining in the simple, loving fashion which makes these home festivals so pleasant at the time, so sweet to remember long afterward, and then all fell to work.

The Christmas Dinner

CHARLES DICKENS

CHRISTMAS TIME! The man must be a misanthrope indeed, in whose breast something like a jovial feeling is not roused—in whose mind some pleasant associations are not awakened—by the recurrence of Christmas. There are people who will tell you that Christmas is not to them what it used to be: that each succeeding Christmas has found some cherished hope, or happy prospect, of the year before, dimmed or passed away, and that the present only serves to remind them of reduced circumstances and straitened incomes—of the feasts they once bestowed on hollow friends, and of the cold looks that meet them now, in adversity and misfortune. Never heed such dismal reminiscences. There are few men who have lived long enough in the world, who cannot call up such thoughts any day in the year. Then do not select the merriest of the three hundred and sixty-five, for your doleful recollections, but draw your chair nearer the blazing fire—fill the glass and send round the song—and if your room be smaller than it was a dozen years ago, or if your glass be filled with reeking punch, instead of sparkling wine, put a good face on the matter, and empty it off-hand, and fill another, and troll off the old ditty you used to sing, and thank God it's no worse. Look on the merry faces of your children as they sit round the fire. One little seat may be empty; one slight form that gladdened the father's heart, and roused the mother's pride to look upon, may not be there. Dwell not upon the past; think not that one short year ago, the fair child now resolving into dust, sat before you, with the bloom of health upon its cheek, and the gay unconsciousness of infancy in its joyous eye. Reflect upon your present blessings—of which every man has many—not on your past misfortunes, of which all men have some. Fill your glass again, with a merry face and contented heart. Our life on it, but your Christmas shall be merry, and your New Year a happy one.

Who can be insensible to the outpourings of good feeling, and the honest interchange of affectionate attachment, which abound at this season of the year? A Christmas family party! We know nothing in nature more delightful! There seems a magic in the very name of Christmas. Petty jealousies and discords are forgotten: social feelings are awakened in bosoms to which they have long been strangers: father and son, or brother and sister, who have met and passed with averted gaze, or a look of cold recognition, for months before, proffer and return the cordial embrace, and bury their past animosities in their present happiness. Kindly hearts that have yearned towards each other, but have been withheld by false notions of pride and self-dignity, are again reunited, and all is kindness and benevolence! Would that Christmas lasted the whole year through, and that the prejudices and passions which deform our better nature, were never called into action among those to whom they should ever be strangers!

The Christmas family party that we mean, is not a mere assemblage of relations, got up at a week or two's notice, originating this year, having no family precedent in the last, and not likely to be repeated in the next. It is an annual gathering of all the accessible members of the family, young or old, rich or poor; and all the children look forward to it, for two months beforehand, in a fever of anticipation. Formerly it was held at Grandpapa's; but Grandpapa getting old, and Grandmamma getting old too, and rather infirm, they have given up housekeeping, and domesticated themselves with Uncle George, so the party always takes place at Uncle George's house, but Grandmamma sends in most of the good things, and Grandpapa always *will* toddle down, all the way to Newgate market, to buy the turkey, which he engages a porter to bring home behind him in triumph, always insisting on the man's being rewarded with a glass of spirits, over and above his hire, to drink "a merry Christmas and a happy New Year" to Aunt George. As to Grandmamma, she is very secret and mysterious for two or three days beforehand, but not sufficiently so to prevent rumors getting afloat that she has purchased a beautiful new cap with pink ribbons for each of the servants, together with sundry books, and penknives, and pencil cases, for the younger branches; to say nothing of diverse secret additions to the order originally given by Aunt George at the pastry cook's, such as another dozen of mince pies for the dinner, and a large plum cake for the children.

On Christmas eve, Grandmamma is always in excellent spirits, and after employing all the children, during the day, in stoning the plums and all that, insists regularly every year on Uncle George coming down into the kitchen, taking off his coat, and stirring the pudding for half an hour or so, which Uncle George good-humoredly does, to the vociferous delight of the children and ser-vants, and the evening concludes with a glorious game of blind-man's-buff, in an early stage of which Grandpapa takes great care to be caught, in order that he may have an opportunity of displaying his dexterity.

On the following morning, the old couple, with as many of the children as the pew will hold, go to church in great state, leaving Aunt George at home dusting decanters and filling castors, and Uncle George carrying bottles into the dining-parlor, and calling for corkscrews, and getting into everybody's way.

When the church party return to lunch, Grandpapa produces a small sprig of mistletoe from his pocket, and tempts the boys to kiss their little cousins under it—a proceeding which affords both the boys and the old gentleman unlimited satisfaction, but which rather outrages Grandmamma's ideas of decorum, until Grandpapa says, that when he was just thirteen years and three months old, *he* kissed Grandmamma under a mistletoe too, on which the children clap their hands, and laugh very heartily, as do Aunt George and Uncle George; and Grandmamma looks pleased, and says, with a benevolent smile, that Grandpapa always was an impudent dog, on which the children laugh very heartily again, and Grandpapa more heartily than any of them.

But all these diversions are nothing to the subsequent excitement when Grandmamma in a high cap, and slate-colored silk gown, and Grandpapa with a beautifully plaited shirt-frill, and white necker-chief, seat themselves on one side of the drawing-room fire, with Uncle George's children and little cousins innumerable, seated in the front, waiting the arrival of the anxiously expected visitors.

Suddenly a hackney-coach is heard to stop, and Uncle George, who has been looking out of the window, exclaims, "Here's Jane!" on which the children rush to the door, and helter-skelter downstairs; and Uncle Robert and Aunt Jane, and the dear little baby, and the nurse, and the whole party, are ushered upstairs amidst tumultuous shouts of "Oh, my!" from the children, and frequently repeated warnings not to hurt baby from the nurse: and Grandpapa takes the child, and Grandmamma kisses her daughter, and the confusion of this first entry has scarcely subsided, when some other aunts and uncles with more cousins arrive, and the grown-up cousins flirt with each other, and so do the little cousins too, for that matter, and nothing is to be heard but a confused din of talking, laughing, and merriment.

A hesitating double knock at the street door, heard during a momentary pause in the conversation, excites inquiry of "Who's that?" and two or three children, who have been standing at the window, announce in a low voice, that it's "poor Aunt Margaret." Upon which Aunt George leaves the room to welcome the new-comer, and Grandmamma draws herself up rather stiff and stately, for Margaret married a poor man without her consent, and poverty not being a sufficiently weighty punishment for her offense has been discarded by her friends, and debarred the society of her dearest relatives.

But Christmas has come round, and the unkind feelings that have struggled against better dispositions during the year, have melted away before its genial influence, like half-formed ice beneath the morning sun. It is not difficult in a moment of angry feeling for a parent to denounce a disobedient child; but to banish her at a period of general goodwill and hilarity, from the hearth round which she has sat on so many anniversaries of the same day, expanding by slow degrees from infancy to girlhood, and then bursting, almost imperceptibly, into the high-spirited and beautiful woman, is widely different. The air of conscious rectitude, and cold forgiveness, which the old lady has assumed, sits ill upon her; and when the poor girl is led in by her sister, pale in looks and broken in spirit—not from poverty, for that she could bear, but from the consciousness of undeserved neglect, and unmerited unkindness— it is easy to see how much of it is assumed. A momentary pause succeeds; the girl breaks suddenly from her sister and throws herself, sobbing, on her mother's neck. The father steps hastily forward, and grasps her husband's hand. Friends crowd round to offer their hearty congratulations, and happiness and harmony again prevail.

As to the dinner, it's perfectly delightful—nothing goes wrong, and everybody is in the very best of spirits, and disposed to please and be pleased. Grandpapa relates a circumstantial account of the purchase of the turkey, with a slight digression relative to the purchase of previous turkeys, on former Christmas days, which Grandmamma corroborates in the minutest particular. Uncle George tells stories, and carves poultry, and takes wine, and jokes with the children at the side table, and winks at the cousins that are making love, or being made love to, and exhilarates everybody with his good humor and hospitality; and when at last a stout servant staggers in with a gigantic pudding, with a sprig of holly in the top, there is such a laughing, and shouting, and clapping of little chubby hands, and kicking up of fat dumpy legs, as can only be equalled by the applause with which the astonishing feat of pouring lighted brandy into mince pies is received by the younger visitors. Then the desert!—and the wine!—and the fun!

Such beautiful speeches, and *such* songs, from Aunt Margaret's husband, who turns out to be such a nice man, and *so* attentive to Grandmamma! Even Grandpapa not only sings his annual song with unprecedented vigor, but on being honored with an unanimous *encore*, according to annual custom, actually comes out with a new one which nobody but Grandmamma ever heard before: and a young scape-grace of a cousin, who has been in some disgrace with the old people, for certain heinous sins of omission and commission—neglecting to call, and persisting in drinking Burton Ale—astonishes everybody into convulsions of laughter by volunteering the most extraordinary comic songs that were ever heard. And thus the evening passes, in a strain of rational goodwill and cheerfulness, doing more to awaken the sympathies of every member of the party in behalf of his neighbor, and to perpetuate their good feeling during the ensuing year, than all the homilies that have ever been written, by all the divines that have ever lived.

A Christmas Prayer

ROBERT LOUIS STEVENSON

Loving Father, help us remember the birth of Jesus, that we may share in the song of the angels, the gladness of the shepherds, and the worship of the wise men.

Close the door of hate and open the door of love all over the world.

Let kindness come with every gift and good desires with every greeting.

Deliver us from evil by the blessing which Christ brings, and teach us to be merry with clear hearts.

May the Christmas morning make us happy to be thy children, and the Christmas evening bring us to our beds with grateful thoughts, forgiving and forgiven, for Jesus' sake. Amen!